Hezekiah Butterworth

Zigzag journeys in Acadia and New France

A summer's journey of the Zigzag Club through the historic fields of the early

French settlements of America

Hezekiah Butterworth

Zigzag journeys in Acadia and New France
A summer's journey of the Zigzag Club through the historic fields of the early French settlements of America

ISBN/EAN: 9783744745154

Printed in Europe, USA, Canada, Australia, Japan

Cover: Foto ©Andreas Hilbeck / pixelio.de

More available books at **www.hansebooks.com**

THE ZIGZAG SERIES

By HEZEKIAH BUTTERWORTH
Of the Editorial Staff of the "Youth's Companion"
and Contributor to "Saint Nicholas" Magazine

Each Volume complete in itself
Now Published
ZIGZAG JOURNEYS
IN EUROPE
IN CLASSIC LANDS
IN THE ORIENT
IN THE OCCIDENT
IN NORTHERN LANDS

NEW
VOLUME
FOR
1881

ZIGZAG JOURNEYS IN ACADIA

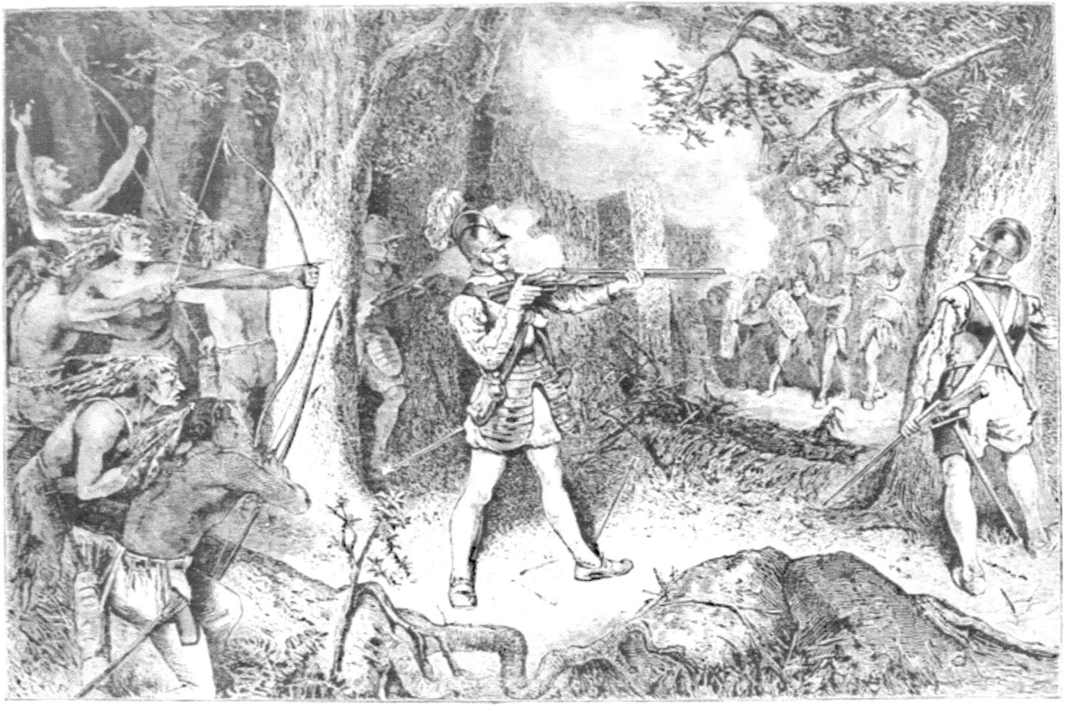

CHAMPLAIN FIGHTING THE INDIANS.

ZIGZAG JOURNEYS

IN

ACADIA

And

NEW FRANCE

A Summer's Journey of the Zigzag Club
through the historic fields of the early
French settlements of AMERICA

by

HEZEKIAH BUTTERWORTH

Author of "Young Folks' History of America,"
"Young Folks' History of Boston,"
"Zigzag Journeys in Europe," etc.

FULLY ILLUSTRATED

BOSTON
ESTES and LAURIAT
301—305 Washington Street
1885

PREFACE.

THE aim of the Zigzag books is to awaken an interest in the history, geography, and political condition of each country of which they treat, by means of a narrative of supposed travel, that makes a visit to interesting places the purpose of the young travellers.

It is hoped that the light narrative, with its pictures, legends, and interpolated stories, may awaken an interest in the young mind that will lead to the reading of more solid books on the same countries and topics, as maturer years follow the story-loving period of youth.

H. B.

CONTENTS.

* —

ILLUSTRATIONS.

CHAPTER I.

A ZIGZAG JOURNEY IN NEW FRANCE (CANADA).

SAMUEL DE CHAMPLAIN'S WONDERFUL STORY AT THE COURT OF FONTAINEBLEAU.

T the opening of the Academy of Yule, Master Lewis, the principal, gave the Class in History the Reigns of Henry IV., Louis XIII., and Louis XIV. of France, as the topic of study for the term.

"This period," he said, "is the most romantic of France. Henry IV. may be called the father of religious liberty. The Edict of Nantes, like the Magna Charta, was one of the greatest events in the history of human progress. It was revoked by Louis XIV., but its lesson and influence were never lost. The study of this period will thrill you with the Battle of Ivry, and give you a view of the dramatic statesmanship of Richelieu, the fall of Rochelle, and the exile of the Huguenots."

He paused; but, the Class giving evidence of interest, he continued: "This, too, was the French period of discovery; your study will make you acquainted with the early history of Canada, or 'New France.' The voyages of Champlain are a romance; Acadia is a

story. and the legends of the St. Lawrence are among the most
poetic of our country. Read Haliburton's 'Nova Scotia;' read all
of Parkman and the first volumes of Bancroft; go to the Boston
Public Library some holiday afternoon, and examine the curious maps
and pictures in the 'Voyages of Champlain;' for a glowing view
of France during the period, take Guizot; for poetry, study 'Evangeline;' for local works, read the 'Chronicles of the St. Lawrence,'
'Maple Leaves,' and 'Picturesque Quebec,' by Le Moine.

"You will find stories in all the histories of this period; and they
will not seem time-worn, but new. You will wonder that the tales
and adventures of the voyagers between the old ports of St. Malo
and Rochelle in Old France and the new ports of the Isle of Orleans. Quebec, and Port Royal in New France should have found
so small a space in romance and poetry. The tales of the St.
Lawrence are as pleasing as those of the Rhine; and if the legends of the river are less wonderful than those of the river of
song, they are at least better supported by facts. I anticipate
that your lessons will be more like pleasing entertainments than
dry tasks."

Master Lewis understood the art of awakening expectation.
Every successful teacher does. He sought to make a subject so
attractive that the pupil would be eager to understand and master it.
He took down the six volumes of Parkman that relate especially
to Canada, and left them on his desk, remarking as he went
out.

You may become so much interested in the study of New
France as to wish to make a Zigzag Journey through the region in
search of the associations of its stories and legends."

The next day the good teacher awakened a more vivid interest
in the subject in the minds of the Class, by introducing the history
lesson by a story that presented a view of a very romantic event
of history.

HENRY IV. AT IVRY.

AFTER-DINNER DIVERSIONS.

CHAMPLAIN'S STORY AT FONTAINEBLEAU.

Let us glance at the history of France at the time of the early settlement of Canada.

Gay was the Court of France during the last days of Henry IV., just before the tragedy. What tragedy?

I see that you ask in the expression of your faces. I will tell you before I leave the subject.

A cloud was hanging over the glowing days of which I shall speak, unseen, but gathering its glooms amid the splendors. You shall hear.

You have a picture of Henry IV. already in your mind. You are all acquainted with Macaulay's noble ballad, "The Battle of Ivry," beginning

> "Now glory to the Lord of Hosts, from whom all glories are;
> And glory to our sovereign liege, King Henry of Navarre!"

Henry IV., surnamed The Great, and also The Good, was the hero of this battle. The battle won for Henry his disputed throne; in my view, it also won for the world religious liberty.

Henry began his reign as a Protestant king; he became a Catholic king; but both as a Protestant and a Catholic he was true to the first principles of human liberty, — to the equal rights of all good people. His hand issued the Edict of Nantes, granting freedom of worship to every soul. A hundred years before Roger Williams taught the principles of religious liberty, Henry IV. of France and Navarre made them facts of history. He issued the Edict of Nantes after he became a Catholic. He was one of the noblest souls in politics that saw the light of France before the Revolution. So, when I hear one of you begin your declamation with

> " Now glory to the Lord of Hosts, from whom all glories are,
> And glory to our sovereign liege, King Henry of Navarre ! "

my heart enters into the spirit of the ballad, and I pay back to the memory of Henry the debt of gratitude that I owe.

Some of you will ask, Was not the Edict of Nantes revoked by Louis XIV., and were not the Protestants exiled from France? Yes, it was revoked, and the Huguenots were dispersed into all civilized lands; but the lesson of that grand decree, like that of England's Magna Charta, was inspiration. We can trace our own religious liberty to it. Its light was obscured, but never went out.

The mother of Henry was a Protestant. She had a heroic soul, and she engaged strong men for his instructors, and inured him to the knightly habits and the rude and common fare of the Bernais mountaineers.

The ballad tells you of Rochelle, "proud city of the waters." From its bright harbor the ships went out on the Bay of Biscay. It was, in the times of which I speak, the stronghold of Protestantism. The mother of Henry one day learned that a plot was on foot to steal her son, take him to Spain, and educate him in the principles she opposed. She hastened to Rochelle, and thrilled the liberal cause by presenting the prince to the assembled Protestant army.

It was a brilliant scene. Condé and Coligny, the great Protestant leaders, had just come to Rochelle, making as it were a providential march. Condé had fled from his castle, taking with him his wife and child, and had crossed the Loire by a ford, singing, "When Israel came out of Egypt." The Protestant hosts flocked to Rochelle; the nobles, the flower of the Huguenot cause.

It announced that the Queen of Navarre was flying towards Rochelle with princes. The great Condé went out to meet her. It was September. Condé and the prince, and led the royal party into the city. It was a day of Rochelle in her glory. Yet the life of nearly every one who engaged in that bright scene ended in a tragedy. Condé fell in battle; Coligny was killed in the Massacre of St. Bartholomew; and the Queen of Navarre is supposed to

CONDÉ AT THE FORD.

have been poisoned. The Protestant nobles were murdered on the night of St. Bartholomew, and Rochelle itself, during the reign of Louis XIII, was levelled to the ground.

The religious wars darkened France. The Catholic and the Huguenot were bent on each other's destruction. It is asserted that at the Massacre of St. Bartholomew sixty thousand people were murdered. The streets of Paris had run with blood as with the torrents of rain that fell in the tempest. The

INDOLENCE OF HENRY III.

reign of the dissolute and indolent Henry III. followed. The Duke of Guise, an intense Catholic partisan, was his enemy. The Catholic party headed by Guise formed the famous Holy League, an organized opposition to Protestantism. The one desire of Henry's heart became the destruction of Guise.

When Coligny was murdered at the Massacre of St. Bartholomew, his body was thrown from the window of his room into the street, and it is said that the Duke of Guise kicked it in the face. He at least gloated in brutal triumph over the dead body of his aged rival. Henry III. plotted the death of Guise, and at last got an assassin to accomplish it. Guise was murdered in the royal palace, to which he had been summoned. The king triumphed over the sight of his corpse, as Guise had done over that of Coligny. Dark days were these.

"I am sole king now," he said to his ministers.

To the queen mother, who was ill, he said, —

"How do you feel?"

"Better."

"So do I. I feel much better. This morning I have become King of France again."

"You have had the Duke of Guise killed then?" asked the invalid.

"Yes."

"Have you reflected well? I hope the cutting is right. Now for the sewing."

His triumph was short.

The Duke of Mayenne, the brother of Guise, became the leader of the League.

In August, 1509, he was told that a monk desired to speak with him.

"Let him in," said the king; "if he is refused, it will be said that I drive monks away and will not see them."

The monk entered, having in his sleeve an unsheathed knife. He bowed to the king, and presented him despatches.

"May I speak with you in private?" he asked.

The king ordered his attendants to retire.

The monk approached the king, and suddenly drove the knife into his body and left it there.

"He has killed me," said the king, drawing out the knife; "kill him!"

The monk stretched out his two arms against the wall in the form of a crucifix, and in this attitude received his death-blow.

The red war between the Catholics and Calvinists went on. Tragedy succeeded tragedy. Henry IV. was now heir to the throne, but his succession was opposed by the Catholic nobles.

The King of Navarre and Mayenne now engaged in a deadly struggle for the royal power.

In the spring of 1590 Henry triumphed over Mayenne and the League at Ivry, on the banks of the Eure.

"Their white standard is in my hands," said Henry, after the battle. "It is a miraculous work of God. To him alone is the glory!"

Henry had rushed into the battle like an inspired hero.

"Soldiers," he said, "I will conquer or die. If your standards fall, do not lose sight of my white plume. You will always find it in the path of honor, and I hope of victory!"

GUISE AND THE CORPSE OF COLIGNY.

In July, 1593, Henry repaired in great pomp to the church of St. Denis. For state reasons he had determined to become a Catholic, and yet to protect the Protestant cause.

"Who are you?" asked the archbishop, as he approached the door of the abbey.

"The king."

"What want you?"

"To be received into the bosom of the Catholic Church."

The archbishop gave him his benediction, and the vaulted roofs rang with the shout, "*Long live the King!*"

"DO NOT LOSE SIGHT OF MY WHITE PLUME."

He issued the Edict of Nantes, giving to all men alike liberty of worship. The wave of war receded, factions lost their force, and France again was happy and at peace. Absolution was given the king by the Pope, and a week after the king and the Duke of Mayenne became friends.

Henry now had liberty to enjoy his beautiful palaces. One of these was at Monceaux, another at St. Germain, and a favorite one at Fontainebleau.

Peace was made with Spain. Sully, a most wise and prudent minister, was given the control of finance, and navigators were sent over the sea to plant the Cross and the Lilies of France in the newly discovered lands.

Charming was the court at Fontainebleau in these golden-tided days; fully

as delightful as the peaceful court of Elizabeth over the Channel. It was enlivened with romances, music, and tales of valor. Courtly men and women, men
of genius, discoverers, adventurers, strangers, all found a ready welcome to the
large hospitalities of Henry.

Among those who visited the gay court at Fontainebleau was a mail-clad
voyager of St. Malo, who had just returned from America. He brought with
him the head of an Iroquois Indian, which excited great curiosity, and pre-

CHAMPLAIN.

sented to the king a belt
of quills of the Canadian
porcupine, and two scarlet
birds, and the skull of a
gar fish.

The weather-beaten
sailor and explorer had
come from the St. Law-
rence, where he had
founded a city and an
empire.

There had been a ban-
quet at Fontainebleau.
Champlain had been a
guest.

"Relate to us the tale
of your adventures," said
the king.

The court gathered
around the dusky hero,
who seemed to the nobles
and ladies like one who
had returned from a fabu-
lous world. The head of
the dead Iroquois had
filled every one with a sense of fear and awe; and silence fell upon the assembly
as the voyager arose and bent low before the king.

After a study of his own narrative I think his story must have been nearly as
follows : —

" May it please your Majesty," said he, " to listen to me for an hour, I will
speak of the people I have met in the Empire of the West. You have received

THE MURDER OF GUISE.

my reports of the River St. Lawrence. Such a river no eye in Europe ever sees. The sun descends into the sea of glass, and seems to remain there like a golden island, while the sky glows like a crimson pavilion, and the birds wheel in dead silence through the dusky air. Nature at that awful hour seems still

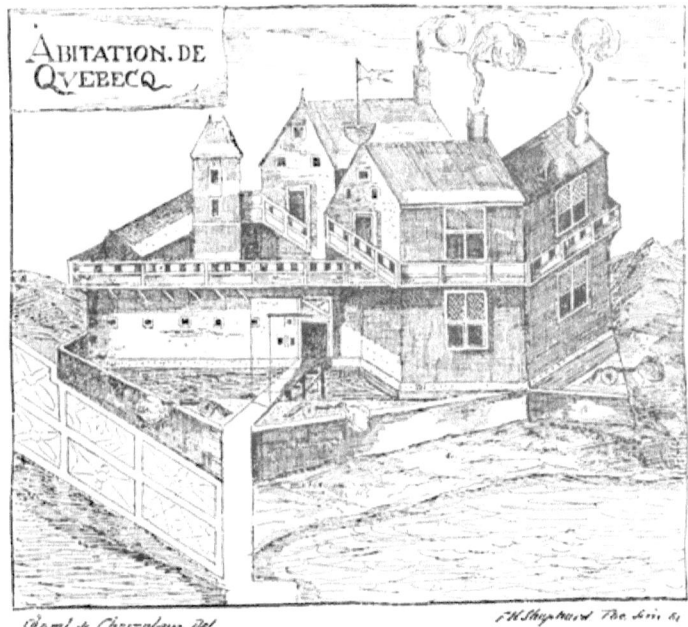

ABITATION. DE QVEBECQ

Saml. de Champlain, del.   F.H.Shepherd. The Scis &c

HABITATION AT QUEBEC.

"You know of the city I have founded, and called Quebec. It is at the foot of a rocky eminence, and by it flows the majestic river. The banks of the river are eternally green with pine. Lofty mountains rise near the city; grand waterfalls and gloomy rivers. The place seems a fit abode for gods rather than men. I have planted an altar to the true God there, to whom be glory forever!

"Beautiful is May in that region. Flowers fill the snows, and the ice goes drifting out of the river. The pines are full of the songs of birds.

"Last May, I made an expedition up this glorious river. I and my companions were clad in armor. We presently came to an Indian village.

"The Indians looked upon us with astonishment. They seemed to think that we were divinities. I asked for their chief. He was sent for, and when he came, he made for us a feast.

"I invited the chief and his warriors to Quebec. They came. I made a feast for them there.

"Amid the festivities I caused an arquebuse and a cannon to be fired. They seemed to think that the reports were thunder peals, and to believe that we controlled the elements.

"The Indians had told me of a wonderful lake in the far forests. It was said to be surrounded with mountains, and as beautiful as Paradise. They wished to conduct me there.

"'We have enemies there,' said the old chief. 'Go fight for us with your weapons of thunder.'

"I promised to go. I well knew that the explosion of an arquebuse would terrify the hearts of their bravest enemies.

"We set out in shallops and canoes. It was June. We passed silent mountains that towered like giants in the serene and resplendent air.

"The old chief gloated in the hope of triumph and revenge.

"'Ugh, ugh! What will the Iroquois do when he hears that?' pointing to an arquebuse. 'Thunder! thunder! He run, run; then all the great land will be mine, the land of the great seas as large as the sky!'

"We came to foaming rapids. The Indians had told me that the route would be over clear water. I sent back our shallops and most of my men to Quebec; then went on with two companions, following the Indian warriors as they dragged overland their canoes.

"On, on we went, — three French champions to contend against the warriors of a great nation.

"'Never fear,' said the chiefs. 'Algonquin no fear. Iroquois will run, run, when he hears the thunder.'

"On, on over marshes, meadows, and streams; through forests over which the air seemed to burn in unchanging splendor. The way was often tangled with flowers. Birds flew from the thickets; eagles screamed overhead.

"Sixty painted warriors carried twenty-four canoes. We marched in silence. At night the medicine-men consulted the spirits.

CASTLE OF ST. GERMAIN IN THE REIGN OF HENRY IV.

"Again upon the water, our canoes glided onward in silence. The river broadened. Islands appeared. I entered a lake, full of islands covered with trees. It was like a wilderness in the sea, a magnificence of water! How glorious it looked upon that summer day, as it glowed under the calm sky! The Indians had not deceived me. I myself would have compared it to a lake of Paradise. What islands, what mountains, what transparency of air, what tranquillity of waters! It was margined with little pines and lilies. Great pines and oaks towered above it on its banks and near hills. Everywhere were birds.

"We travelled by night and slept days, that we might not be seen by the Iroquois. On the 29th of July, after paddling our canoes all night, I lay down to sleep on some spruce boughs. I dreamed. I saw the Iroquois in my dream. They were drowning in the beautiful lake. I hastened to rescue them, when some strange Algonquin Indians appeared to me. 'Do not touch them,' they cried, 'they are of no account ; leave them to their destiny.'

"When I awoke, I related my dream. The Indians declared it a revelation from the Great Spirit, and were filled with hope and joy.

"'The Iroquois cannot stand before *thunder*,' said the chiefs. 'The Iroquois will *scoot*, *scoot*, run like the deer, fly like the partridge, when he hears the white man's thunder!'

"The next night, as we moved on our journey, we discovered dark objects gliding along the waters. They were canoes. As we drew nearer we saw that they were filled with Iroquois. The near boatmen discovered us, and sent up a warning cry. It was answered from boat to boat ; and so fierce were the cries that the lake seemed filled with demons.

"The Iroquois hurried to the shore and began to erect a barricade. The noise of axes rung through the night. An army was gathering. We knew that there would be a battle in the morning.

"Towards morning I put on my armor and made ready my ammunition, then hid myself in my canoe. My French companions did the same. The Iroquois had no suspicion that such champions were among the enemy.

"In the morning, as the light came breaking through the mists of the summer lake, we landed at some distance from the barricade that the Iroquois had built. We had but touched the shore when we beheld the Iroquois warriors, led by plumed chiefs, marching out to meet us. They were tall men, and were covered with a kind of armor made of hardened twigs. They greatly outnumbered our warriors, and they marched with a proud step, like Goliath to meet David.

CULLY.

"Our party surrounded me and my two companions, so that we might not be seen. As the Iroquois came within shooting distance, the braves opened their ranks and left us standing in full view of the Iroquois chiefs.

"I advanced. The Iroquois halted. They gazed upon me with surprise and wonder. They seemed not to comprehend what I was, whether a man, beast, or a god. They stood in utter silence.

"I raised my arquebuse. The movement seemed to surprise them still more. I levelled it. There was a flash and a ringing report. The smoke cleared; and I saw an Iroquois warrior lying dead.

"Our party sent up a cry of triumph, and filled the air with arrows. The Iroquois stood still. They seemed riveted to the ground with amazement at the report of the arquebuse.

"I raised the weapon again. There was another report. Another warrior fell; and as he tumbled over, the Iroquois broke their ranks, and with flying leaps scattered in every direction.

THE CASTLE OF MONCEAUX.

I never saw men run like these Iroquois ; they seemed to vanish.

"Our Indians pursued them, uttering terrific screams. The Iroquois left behind them their camp, canoes, and provisions. Our victory was complete. We returned to Quebec, bringing the heads of three Iroquois warriors.

"One of these I have brought to your Majesty. I assure you it is the head of as stately a warrior as ever strode through the forest. The Iroquois did not run because they thought to save their lives, but because they believed that they were contending with supernatural beings."

Such was substantially one of the narratives of Samuel de Champlain at Fontainebleau.

These narratives delighted the King. He had the voyager relate to him all of his adventures in the New World. The wonders of New France filled his dreams in his last happy days. For they were his last. He was fifty-six years of age. There came upon him a presentiment that he was about to be assassinated.

HENRY IV.

"My friend," he said to Sully, his faithful minister of finance, "I know not what it means, but my heart tells me that something is about to happen to me. I shall die in this city. I have been told that I shall die in my carriage."

On May 14, 1610, the king set out in his carriage for the arsenal, to visit Sully, who was ill. He had been to Mass, and on his return from the church had addressed to two nobles these remarkable words : —

"You do not understand me now, you and the rest. I shall die ; and when you have lost me, you will know my worth, and the difference there is between me and other kings."

"Die?" said Bassompierre, one of the nobles. "You will live years. You are in the flower of your age, full of strength. You have more honors than any mortal man. You live in the most flourishing kingdom in the world. You have a fine family ; you are loved and adored by your subjects."

"My friend," said the king, sadly, "I must leave them all."

That day, on his way toward the arsenal, he was stricken down by an assassin. He received the mortal wound in his carriage, while conversing with two friends. He was taken to the Louvre, and there, without a farewell word, the pacificator of Europe and the author of the Edict of Nantes died. France never wept over any man as over the bier of Henry IV.

I have opened to you the door to the history of Canada, or, as it was called, New France. I have said enough to show you that the Court of Old France had turned its eyes toward the New World. An era of French discovery and conquest was at hand. The old sea-kings of St. Malo and the courtly knights of Normandy were asking for ships. America was the land of mystery. What treasures for the enrichment of the French crown might it contain ! what triumphs for the Church !

Great was the expectation. The Fleur-de-lis and the Cross were ready to march to the empire of the West. The stories of Champlain flew through the provinces. The dream of a new dominion for France glowed in the minds of the nobles and the people. Richelieu, the all-powerful, was about to bend France and Europe to his will, and to aspire to colonize that yet unmapped land, the story of whose wonders was thrilling the world. So began Canada.

CHAPTER II.

A PROPOSED JOURNEY IN SEARCH OF THE STORIES AND LEGENDS
OF NEW FRANCE.

The Story of the Golden Ship, and the Fair Brick House in Green Lane,
Boston.

HE story of Champlain's narrative at the Court of
Henry IV. served the purpose for which it was
intended. It interested the History Class in the
further adventures of the great explorer.

"Was the story a true one?" asked Charlie
Leland of Master Lewis the next day in the study.

"Substantially," said Master Lewis. "It had a framework of
fiction. The incidents of the king and his Court are true. I
followed Guizot. Champlain had an interview with Henry IV. on
his return to France after his first great expedition, and related to
the king and the Court his exploits. I do not know his exact
language; but I gave the story much as I found it in Champlain's
written narrative of his voyage in some of the choicest volumes
of the Boston Public Library, — the same source from which I
suppose Parkman in part gathered his material for the "Pioneers
of France in the New World." One of these books is an English
translation of Champlain's voyages, published by the Prince Society,
of which there are but one hundred and fifty copies. Another is
the official report of the early voyagers to their sovereigns and
patrons, — a so-called G book, which is not allowed to be consulted

except in the Superintendent's department. You will find all of the important and essential facts in Parkman. So you may see that the story as I prepared and framed it was conscientiously done."

"There will be no European tour by members of the Academy next summer?" said Charlie.

"Probably not."

"Why could not the History Class make a journey to Acadia, the St. Lawrence, and the Lakes? We should be prepared for it after studying the history of New France."

"The St. Lawrence," said Master Lewis, "presents to the eye the finest river scenery in America, and perhaps in the world. The Rhine is an infant in size to this giant water-course; but in the romance and antiquity of its legends and history the German stream surpasses the rivers of the world. The Hudson is less beautiful than the St. Lawrence, and the Mississippi less grand.

"The St. Lawrence is not only magnificent in its geographical proportions and its lofty scenery; but the most romantic stories and legends of America are associated with its shores, tributaries, and lakes. The romances of the Indian races are found there. The French period of Canada was the most poetic of American history. Samuel de Champlain was probably the most chivalrous Christian hero that ever set foot on our shores. Every town on the St. Lawrence has its provincial legends and stories. These are to be found in local histories, but are otherwise but little known.

"If the Class could make a journey to Acadia, the St. Lawrence, and the Lakes for the purpose of collecting the stories and legends of the past, it would be likely to prove one of the most interesting tours that could be made in America in summer. It need not be an expensive one, considering that the excursion by water from Picton to Montreal would cover a distance of more than a thousand miles. I think that the excursion fares would not greatly exceed one hundred dollars."

JAMES II.

"What would be the best route, if such a journey could be undertaken?" asked Charlie.

"An historic route, of course. Well, Boston, St. John, Annapolis, Wolfville, and the "Land of Evangeline," Halifax, Cape Breton and Louisburg, Gaspé, the River St. Lawrence, Quebec, Montreal, Lake Champlain, Boston; or, better, from Montreal to Toronto, the Thousand Islands, Niagara, Lake Huron, Lake Superior, to Duluth; thence over the route of Marquette to the Mississippi; thence to the Gulf of Mexico.

"If the shorter route were taken," added Master Lewis, "you could make a détour from Montreal to Ottawa, the Georgian Bay, and the Canadian lakes,—places of historic interest in the settlement of New France. If it were the purpose of the Class to collect the stories and legends of Canada, the pleasing tour would probably make you familiar with much of the history of that country and of France and England. It would bring before you old Port Royal, idyllic Acadia, the New-found-land of the old French voyagers, and Pictou, the industrious town of the great coal-mining region of Nova Scotia, with its lovely harbor, one thousand and fifty miles from Quebec. And here your excursion through the Maritime Provinces of the British Dominion would begin, — an excursion through some fifteen hundred miles of water ways, whose shores are mountains, and whose villages are as romantic as was Grand Pré in vanished Acadia. You would probably take, first, one of the Quebec Steamship Company's steamers which runs between Pictou and Montreal. The fare for this excursion of one thousand miles would be only about thirty dollars.

"On your way you would see Percé, which derives its name from the pierced rock in front of it, and which is as romantic in legends as any rock on the Rhine.

"You might visit Gaspé, where Jacques Cartier landed in 1534, and whose early history is as poetic as its name.

"Massacre Island, the scene of a most tragic event.

"Rimouski, two hundred miles from Quebec, where steamers bound for Europe leave their pilots and take on board the latest mails.

"The Saguenay to Ha Ha Bay, a river as gloomy as the fabled Styx; a cavern rather than a river, dark from mountains of rock that overshadow it; startling and oppressive to-day as it was when Champlain first saw it and described it.

"The island of Orleans, which would fill a book with its old romances.

"Quebec, which in the French provincial days had a highly dramatic history; Point Levi and the Falls of Montmorency, near the town, both of which are as interesting historically; and the St. Lawrence between Quebec and Montreal, which is more beautiful even than the Rhine, the Danube, or the Hudson. I could imagine nothing more delightful than an excursion through this region for the purpose of collecting the stories and legends of Acadia and New France."

The History Class consisted of six bright lads: Herman Reed,

STORM IN HA HA BAY.

Willie Clifton, Louis Robertson, Charlie Noble, Otto Griffiths, and Charlie Leland. Of
these, Herman Reed and Willie Clifton have
figured in previous volumes, and Charlie Leland has before been introduced. Louis Robertson was a favorite in the Class: always
quiet and courteous, but perfectly natural and sincere. He had
heart as well as intellectual worth; everybody was won by him,
and seemed to wish to know him and welcome him, because there
was a certain quiet and courtly sympathy about him, a pleasing

responsiveness that gave his presence a peculiar charm. Noble was his opposite in many respects; of good habits, but inquisitive, a lover of good jokes and comical situations, a popular boy with a nature full of fun. People who played parts in life were all clowns to him, and he liked to ask questions that revealed to them their ignorance and weakness. A dude would have regarded him as a dreadful boy. Master Lewis liked him for his good sense when his judgment was put to the test, although he was often annoyed by certain roguish questions that he asked merely to show his good teacher how limited are human knowledge and reason.

Charlie Leland reported to the Class the questions that he had asked Master Lewis, and the teacher's answers. The subject of an excursion through the territory that once constituted New France, and embraced the eastern coast of the Atlantic, the St. Lawrence, and the Mississippi was discussed, and the purpose of the journey which Master Lewis had suggested, to gain a knowledge of and to collect the stories and legends of New France in America, at once awakened a peculiar interest in the proposed route and the associations of its history. The objection to the plan was that three of the boys would not be able to meet the expenses of such a journey.

"That ought to be no objection," said Charlie Noble. "We can help each other."

"How?" asked Louis Robertson, thoughtfully.

"We can give an exhibition," said Noble; "and those who have money for the excursion can give their part of the profits to those who have not. You, Robertson, can sing; I'll take the comic parts, and we all have talent of some kind or other. It is always easy to get money if one knows how. That's what father says, and I think he knows how, as he began life by sawing wood and now lives on Commonwealth Avenue. I told father one day that our coat of arms ought to be a sawhorse. He smiled, but did not make any answer. I repeated the remark to mother in company, and she did not smile,

but gave me leave of absence and a
cold reception and supper on my
return."

"There are few people who know
how," said Louis.

"It is easy enough," replied Noble,

A DANGEROUS COAST.

with a droll smile on his
freckled face. For example, if you

4

want to make money out of an exhibition, you have just to give the people such an exhibition as the people want. They have their wants, and you have yours, you see.

"You see," he added, "it is just like this, — it is easy enough to fill a want if you know what and where the want is. Now the world is full of wise people and fools. The wise people have the genius to see where the wants are, and they simply make money by filling them; the fools think they know what the wants are, but when they go to supply them they are not there. An exhibition that would please everybody would get everybody's money."

"Suppose you propose such an exhibition," said Louis.

"Well, let us open our eyes. I think that there is a great deal to be gained in this world by keeping one's eyes wide open. Father keeps his eyes open, and yet he says that he has not a dollar that he has not made honestly, and that without injuring any one's honest business or trade.

"Look at the War Song Concert in the city at the Mechanics' Building. There were eight thousand people present. At the same time two of the best musical societies in Boston were giving grand concerts and losing money. Why? The War Song Concert met the wants of the people. The other concerts consisted of programmes that were devoid of popular sympathy. Now the war-song music may have been inferior to the other music; but it met a want, and a right and proper want.

"But how could we meet a want?" asked Louis.

"Well, here is one way. They have concerts of English ballads, Irish ballads, German songs, madrigals, the songs of Bishop, gems from the operas; but who ever heard of a concert of American songs? Now I think that a concert of American songs by a class of young American students would *take*. Why not? The Spanish students have made money out of their concerts. Why should not we?"

That was a subject for further discussion.

Master Lewis, seeing that the story of Champlain had excited so much interest in the study of New France, resolved to add to it by relating other stories of Canada, both in and out of the Class. One of these gave a picture of a period of history with which the boys had little acquaintance, but which prepared the way for a very clear understanding of a part of the subject to which they were now to give their attention.

THE GOLDEN SHIP, AND THE FAIR BRICK HOUSE IN GREEN LANE, BOSTON.

I once heard Charlie Noble say that it is will that makes a fortune, and genius that finds gold ; and that a boy can become anything that he chooses. This is partly true. New England has had few romances. The strangest events that ever happened to any one man in colonial times in New England are those I am about to relate, and will seem to illustrate and confirm Charlie's hopeful and helpful, but somewhat too promising theory.

In the middle of the seventeenth century there lived at Woolwich, in the wilderness of Maine, a family consisting of a man, his wife, and *twenty-six* children. This is not a fairy story.

The family was poor. The children grew up in ignorance. What could a boy out of such a family and such a place ever expect to become?

One of the boys was named William. He was put to tending sheep, and his youth was spent largely in the pastures.

While thus engaged, the beautiful things of nature — the forests, the spring-time, the moon and stars at night — all impressed him with the thought that this was a world of many sides, resources, and opportunities, and that there might be some good fortune in the world for him. He became restless. He was ambitious to learn to read and write.

He bound himself to a ship carpenter at the age of eighteen, and learned of his employer to read and write. He found out from his books that his impression in the pastures was right, that the world *is* wide and full of great opportunities.

In 1673 he came to Boston. He there met a rich lady much older than himself, who took a kindly interest in him and to whom he gave his affections,

Here was an opportunity to secure a good-hearted wife and a fortune at the starting-point, and the young sheep-tender improved his opportunity.

His wife intrusted him with her means; he went into business, and failed, or at least lost all he had, and became as poor as he had been in Maine.

"Never mind, never mind," said he to his wife; "one day I will have a fortune of my own, and then I will make up for all, and I will build you a fair brick house in Green Lane in Boston."

In 1684 this restless young man heard of a Spanish ship that had been lost near the Bahama Islands, and which had contained a large amount of gold and silver. He began to dream of golden ships lying at the bottom of the sea, and to make plans for the recovery of this particular one; and he hoped to build out of the treasure a fair brick house, for his wife, in Green Lane, Boston.

He went to England, full of golden visions. He procured a ship, and went to Bermuda; but he failed to secure the sunken treasure, and returned poor; and Mrs. Phipps must have felt that her prospect of living in a fair brick house was unpromising indeed.

But William still believed in himself. He had chanced, as it would seem, to hear of another Spanish treasure ship, or galleon, that had been cast away near Porto de la Plata. This ship had been freighted with immense riches, and had lain under the waves for fifty years.

William dreamed again. He did not let any feeling of self-depreciation stand in the way of the fulfilment of his plans, and he did not go to idlers with his story, but went boldly to King James, who at that time had great need of money. The king listened to his glowing scheme, and gave him a vessel called the "Rose Algier" to make the attempt to recover the ship of gold.

The golden dreams of one affect others, and the crew of the "Rose Algier" began to dream. They thought that there was a yet shorter way to fortune than searching for sunken ships. It was to capture such ships as they met on the sea. The men advised William to become a pirate.

William would not listen to their proposal. He had an honest heart. The crew mutinied and overcame him; but the ship at last sprung a leak, and he was returned to England, with no nearer prospect of the fair brick house in Green Lane than before.

But he did not lose faith in himself even then. On his last voyage he had met with a Spaniard, an old man, who recalled the place where the Spanish ship had been wrecked. William again went to the king, asked for another vessel, but was refused.

A vessel for the purpose was, however, furnished him by the Duke of Albemarle, who had given an itching ear to William's dreams and schemes. William again sailed from England, and arrived at Porto de la Plata, still thinking, I have no doubt, of the promise he had made to his good wife after losing her fortune, of the fair brick house in Green Lane.

Guided by the directions given by the aged Spaniard, William proceeded to the foaming reef in a boat, taking with him some expert Indian divers. The latter examined the sea-bottom about the reef, but discovered nothing; and doubt and disappointment began to enter our adventurer's heart at last.

The water near the reef was transparent; and William could see the rocks beneath. Looking down into one of the deep crevices of the rocks where the surface was calm, he saw a curious sea-plant, and he said to one of the Indian divers, —

"Go down and bring it up."

The diver plunged. When he came up, he appeared greatly excited.

"What have you found, — gold?"

"No. There are cannon sunken among the rocks."

Cannon! William's heart leaped. He knew that the guns were those of the old Spanish ship.

The English crew danced about the deck at the discovery.

"Down!" said Captain William again to the diver.

Down went all of the divers. They were gone long. They were hunting among the cannon and the old ship's relics. They came up. One of them had a great lump of ore. It proved to be silver, and worth a thousand dollars.

"Thanks be to God!" said Captain William. "Our fortunes are now made!" He doubtless thought of his good wife, and wondered what she would say.

The iron hooks and rakes were put to work. All of the metal and treasure that had formed a part of the galleon and her cargo were brought up. There were bags of gold and silver, plate and jewels of old Spanish grandees, sacks of coin, that broke open upon the deck, and caused the English sailors to shout with delight and to leap about like men demented. In fact, one of the sailors lost his reason, and ever after chatted like an idiot about sunken ships and bags of gold.

The value of the rescued treasure was about $2,000,000. Captain William returned it all honestly to the duke, and the latter gave him, as a reward, a fortune amounting to £16,000, or $80,000.

The king was so much pleased with his perseverance and success that he made him a knight.

He was Sir William Phipps now, and as such was happy to share his good fortune with his lady, who had never dreamed of so much riches and honor.

The Duke of Albemarle sent to Mrs. Phipps a magnificent golden cup; and

OLD PROVINCE HOUSE.

Sir William, as soon as he was able, on returning to America, built for her a fair brick house, in Green Lane, or elsewhere in Boston.

His career was like one of the heroes of the Arabian Nights. The French held Canada, and the French colonies were hostile and dangerous to those of New England. One of the nearest and most interesting of these colonies was Acadia, which has since figured in romance and poetry. Sir William resolved on making an expedition, in the interest of England, to conquer and render powerless this colony; and he hoped also to add to his riches and fame. He was successful; and when he returned to Boston, there was no man in the colony more distinguished than Sir William Phipps.

But his greatest honor was yet to come. William and Mary came to the English throne. England was still hostile to France and her colonies; and when it fell to the new king to appoint a governor for Massachusetts, whom should he commission but the super-serviceable hero of Acadia, Sir William Phipps?

So in the old Province House Sir William sat down in knee-breeches, and ruffles, and waistcoat bedizened with gold, gorgeous as one of the old Spanish grandees whose treasure he had gained; and by him sat Lady Phipps, as resplendent as a court duchess, and very proud of her husband.

Sheep-tender Phipps, Carpenter Phipps, Captain Phipps, Sir William Phipps, Governor Phipps, General Phipps, died suddenly, in England, at the age of forty-four or five. I have told you his story on account of its association with Acadia.

You may hear of him again, should you spend some days on your proposed journey in Quebec. Sir William was not able to accomplish all that he wished ; he was once ambitious to capture the Fortress of Quebec, and attempted it, but had to retire. Still I cannot say what he might have done had he persevered.

" Wolfe accomplished it at last," said Charlie Noble.

" Yes," said Master Lewis. " Suppose you tell us, at some future recitation, who told him how."

CHAPTER III.

HE study of the history of Old and New France during the period of American discovery and settlement made the Class daily more eager to make a summer tour through the Province.

"I shall go," said Charlie Noble, "if I have to ride on a velocipede. I have been thinking about the plan I proposed for a concert of American songs. I think that we could arrange such a concert and make it pay well. If we were successful here, we might repeat it in the cities of the Provinces. When we had spent our money we could sing."

"If we were sure of finding audiences to listen," said Robertson.

"Sure? Make up a programme of songs that people want to hear, and you may be sure of an audience. Any man who has produce that people want to buy is sure of a market. As I said before, my idea of genius is that it is simply knowing how to meet a want. 'He is a genius,' Emerson says, 'who gives me back my own thoughts.'"

"Well, I hope you may prove a genius," said Charlie Leland. "Have you talked with Master Lewis about this matter?"

"Yes."

"What did he say?"

"He said that he would be sorry to see the names of his boys posted about the streets on hand-bills like circus riders."

"Did he say that?"

"Yes; and he said that he had noticed that when boys become used to the public platform they are apt to be restless for noise and applause afterwards and dissatisfied with the plain duties of life. 'I have seen,' said he, 'several good schools ruined by exhibitions;' and he further informed me that 'modesty and public applause are not brothers.'"

"That was rather discouraging," said Robertson. "What did you say in reply?"

"I just said I thought that our plan could not be open to these objections; that there were *enterprise* and *self-reliance* in it, and that *American* songs were *manly things.*

"Now, boys," continued Noble, "there is a great deal in the art of putting things. Why, I once read of an old Egyptian king that dreamed that his teeth dropped out, and he

"ALL YOUR RELATIONS WILL DIE BEFORE YOU."

went to an astrologer for an interpretation of the meaning of his dream. 'It means,' said the astrologer, 'that all your relations will die before you.' The king was very much offended at the interpretation. You see that astrologer did n't know how to interpret. Then the king chanced to meet a poor shepherd by the seaside, and he asked him for an interpretation. The shepherd was bright. 'It means, said he, 'that you shall *outlive* all of your relations.' *That* made the king happy. *Outlive* was just the word.

"I think I said just the right thing to Master Lewis when I spoke of *enterprise, self-reliance,* and of *American songs* being *manly.* He said pleasantly, 'There are two sides to a shield;' and added, 'Give a private concert of American songs in the hall, and I will advise you further when I have heard it.' He said, 'I like your spirit;' that means, 'yes.'

"I propose that the topic for discussion at the next meeting of the Zigzag Club be American songs, and that each member who can sing

be asked to sing an historic song or ballad that relates to our own country. I believe that American boys should be American."

The Zigzag Club was a school society that had been continued in the Academy for many years. Its object, beyond mere entertainment, was to

"YOU WILL OUTLIVE ALL YOUR RELATIONS."

gather information about particular countries, institutions, or places. Charlie Leland *this* year was the president of the Club.

At the meeting of the Club after this discussion, it was voted that the topic of the weekly meetings for a time should be "Stories of Acadia," and that the Musical Committee should arrange for the singing of American songs between the provincial narratives.

Charlie Noble threw his whole soul into the musical plan. He induced Charlie Leland, the school poet, to write original words for the stirring tune known as "The Red, White, and Blue," and also to put into verse a somewhat original ode entitled "So say we all of us," to close the exercises.

THE SONGS AND STORIES OF THE CLUB.

The meeting of the Club to relate stories of Acadia was opened by the song composed by Charlie Leland. The solos were sung by Otto, and the chorus by the musical society of the school. The Club and their friends were somewhat surprised when Otto appeared bearing in his hand a flagstaff with a half-unfolded flag.

TO THE RIGHT, TO THE RIGHT EVER TRUE.

Wake the song to the nation's defenders,
  The years of prosperity glow;
The natal day welcome, that renders
  The love that to valor we owe.
Wake the song where our fathers, undaunted,
  Proclaimed, when the nation was new,
That their ensign for Liberty planted
  Should be to the Right ever true!

CHORUS.

To the Right, to the Right ever true,
To the Right, to the Right ever true,
  The ensign for Liberty planted
Should be to the Right ever true.

When the Red Cross of England contended
  With the Lilies of France, in their might
Our fathers arose and defended
  For freedom the cause of the Right.
Then dared they the sceptre to sever;
  For the Right, the far forest ways trod,
And templed the fair hills wherever
  Their faces were lifted to God.

CHORUS.

To the Right, to the Right ever true,
To the Right, to the Right ever true,
  The ensign for Liberty planted
Has been to the Right ever true.

The banners of tyranny faded, —
    The Red Cross, and Lilies of Gold, —
And the folds no oppression had shaded —
    The stars of the empire — unrolled !
And they pledged it, these heroes victorious,
    As on Liberty's breeze it unfurled,
To the birthright of man, ever glorious,
    And to freemen, the kings of the world !

CHORUS.

To the Right, to the Right ever true,
To the Right, to the Right ever true,
    The ensign for Liberty planted
    Has been to the Right ever true.

Her red war when Slavery vaunted,
    The heroes of Right rose as one ;
The banner the father had planted
    Was guarded for Right by the son.
Young martyrs, — let valor deplore them, —
    Their names on the white marbles glow ;
The roses of June redden o'er them,
    The war bugles peacefully blow.

CHORUS.

To the Right, to the Right ever true,
To the Right, to the Right ever true,
    The Flag they defended, forever
    To the cause of the Right shall be true.

Again, at this altar that binds us,
    The faith of the past we 'll renew,
An hundred years fading behind us,
    A thousand years rising to view.
And as long as the fair constellations
    Shall lighten the heavens with gold,
Shall the banner of Right be the nation's,
    And ever for Right be unrolled !

CHORUS.

To the Right, to the Right ever true,
To the Right, to the Right ever true,
    The flag of our nation forever
    To the cause of the Right shall be true.

Charlie Leland began the story-telling with a brief account of

GLOOSCAP.

The Indians, he said, imagined that their deities dwelt amid beautiful scenery. The top of Mount Washington was believed by them to be a Paradise, and they thought that it was wicked to ascend the mountain beyond a certain limit.

Glooscap was the god of the Micmacs, the Indian tribe of Nova Scotia. His throne was Blomidon.

He was believed to be a Spirit of Universal Good. He assumed the form of a man for the welfare of the Indian race; but he was of heavenly origin, and invulnerable, and not subject to sickness or the law of death. We are told that he dwelt at times above, in a great wigwam, in the realms of effulgent light and illimitable space, — those quiet paradises where the Indian thinks the streams softly flow, and gorgeous birds sing low, and the groves wave in noiseless air; where all things are such as we find them in dreams.

The Indian doctrine was that this deity was "never far from any one who followed his counsel," which was the law of right; so, when any good person was treated with injustice, he appeared in his behalf, assuming some earthly form.

It was he who planted agates around Blomidon, who taught the people to hunt and fish. He governed the spirits of the forest. The animals were a part of his kingdom, as well as spirits and men. In his Golden Age he talked with the animals, and the animals talked with each other.

He had huge hunting-dogs. They were agents of his power.

When the English came, he departed. He turned his two hunting-dogs into stones. There are many stones around Blomidon, — more stones than agates. Two of these are said to be Glooscap's dogs.

He will come again one day. The animals are all expecting him. The white owl has been a solitary bird since he departed, and calls for him in the lonely forests all the night. She says continually, "I am sorry!"

When he comes again he will awaken his two stone dogs. So the Indians once believed. But the Micmacs are becoming a good Christian people, and the superstition is fading away among the myths of the past.

I will read you a poem about Glooscap written by a young clergyman whose early home was in Acadia: —

THE LEGEND OF GLOOSCAP.

Bathed in the sunshine still, as of yore,
Stretches the peaceful Acadian shore;
Fertile meadows and fields of grain
Smile as they drink the summer rain.

There, like a sentinel grim and gray,
Blomidon stands at the head of the Bay;
And the famous Fundy tides, at will,
Sweep into Minas Basin still.

With wondrous beauty the Gaspereaux
Winds its way to the sea below;
And the old Acadian Grand Pré
Is the home of prosperous men to-day.

The place where Basil the blacksmith wrought
In the glow of his forge, is a classic spot;
And every summer tourists are seen
In the fairy haunts of Evangeline.

But the old Acadian woods and shores,
Rich in beautiful legend stores,
Were once the home of an older race,
Who wove their epics with untaught grace.

Long ere the dikes that guard for aye
From the merciless tides the old Grand Pré,
Built by the Frenchman's tireless hands,
Grew round the rich Acadian lands, —

The Micmac sailed in his birch canoe
Over the Basin calm and blue;
Speared the salmon, — his heart's desire;
Danced and slept by his wigwam fire;

Far in the depth of the forest gray
Hunted the moose the livelong day;
While the mother sang to her Micmac child
Songs of the forest weird and wild.

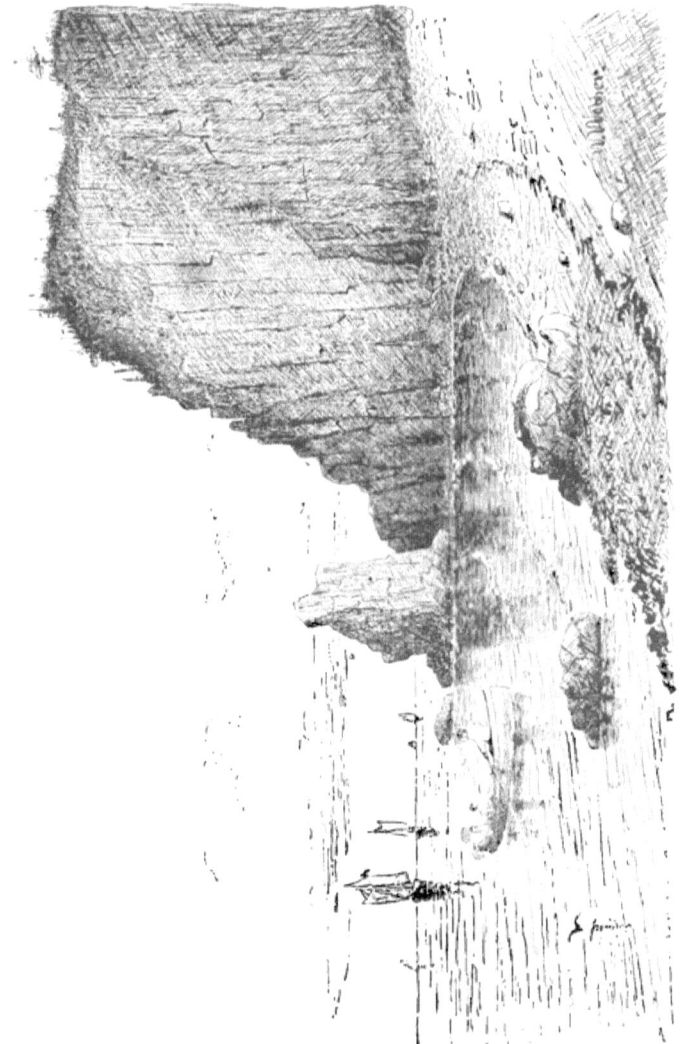

THE THRONE OF GLOOSCAP.

Over the tribe, with jealous eye,
Watched the Great Spirit from on high,
While on the crest of Blomidon
Glooscap, the God-man, dwelt alone.

No matter how far his feet might stray
Far from the haunts of his tribe away,
Glooscap could hear the Indian's prayer,
And send some message of comfort there.

Glooscap it was who taught the use
Of the bow and spear, and who sent the moose
Into the Indian hunter's hands, —
Glooscap, who strewed the shining sands

Of the tide-swept beach of the stormy bay
With amethysts purple and agates gray,
And brought to each newly wedded pair
The Great Spirit's benediction fair.

But the white man came, and with ruthless hand
Cleared the forest, and sowed the land,
And drove from their haunts by the sunny shore
Micmac and moose forevermore.

And Glooscap, saddened and sore distressed,
Took his way to the unknown West;
And the Micmac kindled his wigwam fire
Far from the grave of his child and his sire, —

Where now, as he weaves his basket gay,
And paddles his birch canoe away,
He dreams of the happy time for men,
When Glooscap shall come to his tribe again.

Tommy Toby, an old member of the Club, who used to entertain it, when he was a member of the Academy, with curious historic stories, was present, and had been asked to offer a humorous story.

5

In response to the request, he had merely said, " I do not know any stories of Acadia except ' Evangeline ' and the Skipper's Wild-Geese Eggs." " Tell us the story of the Skipper's Wild-Geese Eggs," said Charlie ; and Tommy had promised to oblige him.

A THANKSGIVING DINNER THAT FLEW AWAY.

There is one sound, said Tommy, that I shall always remember.   It is " Honk ! "

I spun around like a top, one summer day when I heard it, looking nervously in every direction.

I had just come down from the city to the Cape with my sister Hester for my third summer vacation.   I had left the cars with my arms full of bundles, and hurried toward Aunt Targood's.

The cottage stood in from the road.   There was a long meadow in front of it.   In the meadow were two great oaks and some clusters of lilacs.   An old, mossy stone wall protected the grounds from the road, and a long walk ran from the old wooden gate to the door.

It was a sunny day, and my heart was light.   The orioles were flaming in the old orchards ; the bobolinks were tossing themselves about in the long meadows of timothy, daisies, and patches of clover.   There was a scent of new-mown hay in the air.

In the distance lay the bay, calm and resplendent, with white sails and specks of boats.   Beyond it rose Martha's Vineyard, green and cool and bowery, and at its wharf lay a steamer.

I was, as I said, light-hearted.   I was thinking of rides over the sandy roads at the close of the long, bright days ; of excursions on the bay ; of clambakes and picnics.

I was hungry ; and before me rose visions of Aunt Targood's fish dinners, roast chickens, and berry pies.   I was thirsty ; but ahead was the old wellsweep, and behind the cool lattice of the dairy window were pans of milk in abundance.

I tripped on toward the door with light feet, lugging my bundles and beaded with perspiration, but unmindful of all discomforts in the thought of the bright days and good things in store for me.

" Honk ! honk ! "

My heart gave a bound !

Where did that sound come from ?

Out of a cool cluster of innocent-looking lilac bushes, I saw a dark object cautiously moving. It seemed to have no head. I knew, however, that it had a head. I had seen it ; it had seized me once on the previous summer, and I had been in terror of it during all the rest of the season.

I looked down into the irregular grass, and saw the head and a very long neck running along on the ground, propelled by the dark body, like a snake running away from a ball. It was coming toward me, and faster and faster as it approached.

I dropped my bundles.

In a few flying leaps I returned to the road again, and armed myself with a stick from a pile of cord-wood.

"Honk! honk! honk!"

It was a call of triumph. The head was high in the air now. My enemy moved grandly forward, as became the monarch of the great meadow farmyard.

HONK.

I stood with beating heart, after my retreat.

It was Aunt Targood's gander.

How he enjoyed his triumph, and how small and cowardly he made me feel !

"Honk! honk! honk!"

The geese came out of the lilac bushes, bowing their heads to him in admiration. Then came the goslings, — a long procession of awkward, half-feathered things ; they appeared equally delighted.

The gander seemed to be telling his admiring audience all about it : how a strange lad with many bundles had attempted to cross the yard ; how he had driven him back, and had captured his bundles, and now was monarch of the field. He clapped his wings when he had finished his heroic story, and sent forth such a " Honk !" as might have startled a major-general.

Then he, with an air of great dignity and coolness, began to examine my baggage.

Among my effects were several pounds of chocolate caramels, done up in brown paper. Aunt Targood liked caramels, and I had brought her a large supply.

He tore off the wrappers quickly. He bit one. It was good. He began to distribute the bonbons among the geese, and they, with much liberality and good-will, among the goslings.

This was too much. I ventured through the gate, swinging my cord-wood stick.

"Shoo!"

He dropped his head on the ground, and drove it down the walk in a lively waddle toward me.

"*Shoo!*"

It was Aunt Targood's voice at the door.

He stopped immediately.

His head was in the air again.

"*Shoo!*"

Out came Aunt Targood with her broom.

She always corrected the gander with her broom. If I were to be whipped, I should choose a broom, — not the stick.

As soon as he beheld the broom he retired, although with much offended pride and dignity, to the lilac bushes; and the geese and goslings followed him.

"Hester, you dear child," she said to my sister, "come here. I was expecting you, and had been looking out for you, but missed sight of you. I had forgotten all about the gander."

We gathered up the bundles and the caramels. I was light-hearted again.

How cool was the sitting-room, with the woodbine falling about the open windows!

Aunt brought me a pitcher of milk and some strawberries, some bread and honey, and a fan.

While I was resting and taking my lunch, I could hear the gander discussing the affairs of the farmyard with the geese. I did not greatly enjoy the discussion. His tone of voice was very proud, and he did not seem to be speaking well of me.

I was suspicious that he did not think me a very brave lad. A young person likes to be spoken well of, even by the gander.

Aunt Targood's gander had been the terror of many well-meaning people, and of some evil-doers, for many years. I have seen tramps and pack-pedlers enter the gate, and start on toward the door, when there would sound that ringing warning like a war-blast, "Honk, honk!" and in a few minutes these unwelcome people would be gone. Farm-house boarders from the city would sometimes enter the yard, thinking to draw water by the old well-sweep; in a few minutes it was customary to hear shrieks, and to see women and children flying over the walls, followed by air-rending "Honks!" and jubilant cackles from the victorious gander and his admiring family.

Aunt Targood sometimes took summer boarders. Among those that I remember was the Rev. Mr. Bonney, a fervent-souled Methodist preacher. He put the gander to flight with the cart-whip, on the second day after his arrival, and seemingly to aunt's great grief ; but he never was troubled by the feathered tyrant again.

Young couples sometimes came to Father Bonney to be married ; and, one summer afternoon, there rode up to the gate a very young couple, whom we afterward learned had " run away," or, rather, had attempted to get married without their parents' approval. The young bridegroom hitched the horse, and helped from the carriage the gayly dressed miss he expected to make his wife. They started up the walk upon the run, as though they expected to be followed, and haste was necessary to prevent the failure of their plans.

" Honk ! "

They stopped. It was a voice of authority.

" Just look at him ! " said the bride. " Oh ! oh ! "

The bridegroom cried " Shoo ! " but he might as well have said " Shoo " to a steam-engine. On came the gander, with his head and neck upon the ground. He seized the lad by the calf of his leg, and made an immediate application of his wings. The latter seemed to think he had been attacked by dragons. As soon as he could shake him off, he ran. So did the bride, but in another direction ; and while the two were thus perplexed and discomfited, the bride's father appeared in a carriage, and gave her a most forcible invitation to ride home with him. She accepted it without discussion. What became of the bridegroom, or how the matter ended, we never knew.

" Aunt, what makes you keep that gander, year after year ? " said I, one evening, as we were sitting on the lawn before the door. " Is it because he is a kind of watch-dog, and keeps troublesome people away ? "

" No, child, no ; I do not wish to keep most people away, — not well-behaved people, — nor to distress nor annoy any one. The fact is, there is a story about that gander that I do not like to speak of to every one, — something that makes me feel tender toward him ; so that if he needs a whipping, I would rather do it. He knows something that no one else knows. I could not have him killed or sent away. You have heard me speak of Nathaniel, my oldest boy ? "

" Yes."

" That is his picture in my room, you know. He was a good boy to me. He loved his mother. I loved Nathaniel, — you cannot think how much I loved Nathaniel. It was on my account that he went away.

" The farm did not produce enough for us all, — Nathaniel, John, and me.

We worked hard, and had a hard time. One year — that was ten years ago — we were sued for our taxes.

"'Nathaniel,' said I, 'I will go to taking boarders.'

"Then he looked up to me and said, — oh, how noble and handsome he appeared to me! —

"'Mother, I will go to sea.'

"'Where?' asked I, in surprise.

"'In a coaster.'

"I turned white. How I felt!

"'You and John can manage the place,' he continued. 'One of the vessels sails next week, — Uncle Aaron's; he offers to take me.'

"It seemed best, and he made preparations to go.

"The spring before, Skipper Ben — you have met Skipper Ben — had given me some goose eggs; he had brought them from Canada, and said that they were wild-goose eggs.

"I set them under hens. In four weeks I had three goslings. I took them into the house at first, but afterward made a pen for them out in the yard. I brought them up myself, and one of those goslings is that gander.

"Skipper Ben came over to see me, the day before Nathaniel was to sail. Aaron came with him.

"I said to Aaron, —

"'What can I give to Nathaniel to carry to sea with him to make him think of home? Cake, preserves, apples? I have n't got much; I have done all I can for him, poor boy.'

"Brother looked at me curiously, and said, —

"'Give him one of those wild geese, and we will fatten it on shipboard and will have it for our Thanksgiving dinner.'

"What Brother Aaron said pleased me. The young gander was a noble bird, the handsomest of the lot; and I resolved to keep the geese to kill for my own use, and to give *him* to Nathaniel.

"The next morning — it was late in September — I took leave of Nathaniel. I tried to be calm and cheerful and hopeful. I watched him as he went down the walk with the gander struggling under his arms. A stranger would have laughed, but I did not feel like laughing; it was true that the boys who went coasting were usually gone but a few months, and came home hardy and happy. But when poverty compels a mother and son to part, after they have been true to each other, and shared their feelings in common, it seems hard, — it seems hard, though I do not like to murmur or complain at anything allotted to me.

" I saw him go over the hill. On the top he stopped and held up the gander. He disappeared ; yes, my own Nathaniel disappeared. I think of him now as one who disappeared.

" November came. It was a terrible month on the coast that year. Storm followed storm ; the sea-faring people talked constantly of wrecks and losses. I could not sleep on the nights of those high winds. I used to lie awake thinking over all the happy hours I had lived

" I SAW HIM GO OVER THE HILL."

with Nathaniel.

" Thanksgiving week came.

" It was full of an Indian-summer brightness after the long storms. The nights were frosty, bright, and calm.

" I could sleep on those calm nights.

" One morning, I thought I heard a strange sound in the woodland pasture.

It was like a wild goose. I listened; it was repeated. I was lying in bed. I started up, — I thought I had been dreaming.

"On the night before Thanksgiving I went to bed early, being very tired. The moon was full; the air was calm and still. I was thinking of Nathaniel, and I wondered if he would indeed have the gander for his Thanksgiving dinner; if it would be cooked as well as I would have cooked it, and if he would think of me that day.

"I was just going to sleep when suddenly I heard a sound that made me start up and hold my breath.

"'Honk!'

"I thought it was a dream followed by a nervous shock.

"'Honk! honk!'

"There it was again, in the yard. I was surely awake and in my senses.

"I heard the geese cackle.

"'Honk! honk! honk!'

"I got out of bed and lifted the curtain. It was almost as light as day. Instead of two geese there were three. Had one of the neighbors' geese stolen away?

"I should have thought so, and should not have felt disturbed, but for the reason that none of the neighbors' geese had that peculiar call, — that horn-like tone that I had noticed in mine.

"I went out of the door.

"The *third* goose looked like the very gander I had given Nathaniel. Could it be?

"I did not sleep. I rose early and went to the crib for some corn.

"It was a gander — a 'wild' gander — that had come in the night. He seemed to know me.

"I trembled all over as though I had seen a ghost. I was so faint that I sat down on the meal-chest.

"As I was in that place, a bill pecked against the door. The door opened. The strange gander came hobbling over the crib-stone and went to the corn-bin. He stopped there, looked at me, and gave a sort of glad "Honk," as though he knew me and was glad to see me.

"I was certain that he was the gander I had raised, and that Nathaniel had lifted into the air when he gave me his last recognition from the top of the hill.

"It overcame me. It was Thanksgiving. The church bell would soon be ringing as on Sunday. And here was Nathaniel's Thanksgiving dinner; and Brother Aaron's, — had it flown away? Where was the vessel?

"Years have passed, — ten. You know I waited and waited for my boy to come back. December grew dark with its rainy seas; the snows fell; May lighted up the hills, but the vessel never came back. Nathaniel — my Nathaniel — never returned.

"HE NEVER RETURNED."

"That gander knows something he could tell me if he could talk. Birds have memories. *He* remembered the corn-crib, — he remembered something else. I wish he *could* talk, poor bird! I wish he could talk. I will never sell him, nor kill him, nor have him abused. *He knows!*"

Tommy Toby's story of old Malabune and Acadia was followed by a spirited rendering of a Revolutionary song written in or about the year 1769.

THE LIBERTY SONG.

Come, join hand in hand, brave Americans all, And rouse your bold hearts at fair Liberty's call. No tyrannous acts shall suppress your just claim, Or stain with dishonor America's name. In freedom we're born, and in freedom we'll live: Our purses are ready; Steady, friends, steady! Not as slaves, but as freemen, our money we'll give.

Come, join hand in hand, brave Americans all,
And rouse your bold hearts at fair Liberty's call;
No tyrannous acts shall suppress your just claim,
Or stain with dishonor America's name.
In freedom we 're born, and in freedom we 'll live:
　　　Our purses are ready;
　　　Steady, friends, steady!
Not as slaves, but as freemen, our money we 'll give.

Our worthy forefathers — let 's give them a cheer —
To climates unknown did courageously steer:
Through oceans to deserts for freedom they came,
And, dying, bequeathed us their freedom and fame.
　　　　　　　　In freedom we 're born, etc.

Their generous bosoms all dangers despised,
So highly, so wisely, their birthrights they prized;
We 'll keep what they gave, we will piously keep,
Nor frustrate their toils on the land and the deep.
　　　　　　　　In freedom we 're born, etc.

The tree their own hands had to Liberty reared
They lived to behold growing strong and revered:
With transport they cried, "Now our wishes we gain,
For our children shall gather the fruits of our pain."
　　　　　　　　In freedom we 're born, etc.

Swarms of placemen and pensioners soon will appear,
Like locusts, deforming the charms of the year:
Suns vainly will rise, showers vainly descend,
If we are to drudge for what others shall spend.
　　　　　　　　In freedom we 're born, etc.

Then join hand in hand, brave Americans all:
By uniting, we stand; by dividing, we fall.
In so righteous a cause let us hope to succeed;
For Heaven approves of each generous deed.
　　　　　　　　In freedom we 're born, etc.

All ages shall speak with amaze and applause
Of the courage we 'll show in support of our laws;
To die we can bear, — but to serve we disdain;
For shame is to freemen more dreadful than pain.
　　　　　　　　In freedom we 're born, etc.

This bumper I crown for our sovereign's health,
And this for Britannia's glory and wealth :
That wealth and that glory immortal may be,
If she is but just and if we are but free.
In freedom we 're born, and in freedom we 'll live :
　　Our purses are ready :
　　Steady, friends, steady !
Not as slaves, but as freemen, our money we 'll give.

Herman Reed related a very curious historical incident : —

ANNO MURIUM, — THE YEAR OF THE MICE.

In 1699 Dierville, a provincial chronicler, said : "Prince Edward's Island has a plague of mice or locusts every seven years." The mouse plague is a bygone misfortune in the Provinces. It once caused great distress from time to time, not only in Prince Edward's Island, but at Pictou, Colchester, and Antigonish.

In the spring of 1815 a mouse plague fell upon Pictou and the surrounding country, so that, instead of one Bishop Hatto, there were hundreds, though the victims had not, like the cruel bishop of the Rhine, been guilty of any great misdeeds, and they had an easier escape.

The warm air of May loosened the frost ; and just at the time that the earth usually sends forth her flowers, she sent forth instead, to the astonishment of all good people, *mice.* The earth seemed full of mice. There were mouse-holes in all the woods and fields.

Where the early violets had bloomed there were the eyes and noses of hungry mice. The farmer went out to his barn ; mice scampered off before him and followed after him. When he went to feed his pigs he would find the trough full of mice. The farmer's wife found them in her cellar, closet, and sleeping-room. Cats and dogs guarded the barns ; but they often retreated before the attacks of the multitudinous foe.

They were not ordinary mice, small and timid, but were large and bold. They are said to have resembled rats more closely than their own species.

As the days grew warmer, their numbers seemed to increase. They were as thick as grasshoppers in August. They devoured every eatable thing that was not protected by watchfulness and force.

The farmers would go out to plant their fields. The next morning they would find whatever they had put into the ground had been devoured by the mice. Corn, grain, and vegetables alike disappeared.

There was a farmer in Merigomish, a bright, thrifty, enterprising man, who expected to add to his yearly income by raising a fine crop of oats.

He prepared his field; and one morning he put his sacks on board his wagon, and, filling a large measure from the sacks in arriving at the field, he went out to sow.

He marched forward like a general; he scattered the oats to the right and left, in the usual way; and when the oats in his measure were exhausted, he turned about to replenish the measure from a sack in the wagon.

What was his astonish-

ment to find an army of mice at his heels! He was greatly enraged. He strode back over the ground, but only husks of all the oats he had sown remained.

He cut down a young birch-tree, and made war on the mice. He drove them into the walls and woods, and was at last, as he thought, master of the field.

He began to sow again, and continued the work during the morning. At noon he went home for his dinner and more oats. When he returned to his field, it seemed, like the wood in " Macbeth," to be moving. Of all the oats he had sown in the morning, not one was left.

At last the mice began to die for want of food. Fields were covered with them. The air was full of a sickening odor. The starving vermin in many places moved toward the sea-coast in vast numbers, as there was an abundance of shell-fish there. When they had devoured all the shell-fish they could find, they died there, and the tides carried them away.

The mice not only ate the fish, but the larger fish ate the mice. The large fish caught in the bays were found to have mice in their maws.

It is said that there are old people living to-day who remember the Year of the Mice. It was a custom for many years to speak of marriages, births, and deaths as occurring on such or such a date before or after the Year of the Mice. Browning's story " The Pied Piper of Hamelin " is a fiction, as is also Southey's " Bishop Hatto ; " but this story is substantially true, and yet it has found no poet.

" I am not a story-teller," said Willie Clifton, " but I have found a story of the Provinces that has greatly interested me. It is told in a book called " Tales of the St. Lawrence," written by Gardner B. Chapin, and published in Montreal. In relating the story I shall use in part the language of the author.

A FRIGHTENED CAPTAIN.

I once heard a story of a company of Home Guards in a Kentucky town. They met for parade under a pompous and ambitious captain. The object of the organization was to protect the town from Morgan's bands of foragers.

" Shoulder arms ! " said he, imperiously. " Ground arms ! " as loftily.

A negro appeared leaping into the parade ground, out of breath, but swinging his hat.

" Morgan — is — coming," he stammered.

The captain gave one glance at his company, and shouted, " Break ranks ! " and break ranks they did, each seeking his own safety.

It is a somewhat similar story that I find in the entertaining book of which I have spoken.

William Johnson was one of the so-called order of the "Liberators of Canada." A provisional government had been formed, and he had been appointed Commander of the Fleet.

On the night of the 29th of May, 1838, says Chapin, the English passenger steamer "Sir Robert Peel," while on a trip up the river, stopped at a wooding-station on Wells' Island, near the head of the stream; here it was boarded by Johnson, at the head of a score or more of well-armed men, disguised in Indian costume, who at once proceeded to put the passengers and crew, about forty in number, ashore, and then to fire the boat, which was soon burned to the water's edge. This act of hostility towards one government and the violation of the neutrality of the other was productive of great excitement,—a reward was offered by the Governor of the State of New York for his apprehension, and strenuous efforts were made by the British military authorities to effect his capture.

When closely pursued, Johnson had a secret place of retreat, that for a long time served as a place of concealment, and the knowledge of the locality of which was known but to himself and a few of his most trusted confederates. This was a cavern upon one of the almost innumerable islands of the archipelago of the river, sufficiently capacious to serve as a place of residence and concealment for a score of men, and whose entrance it was very difficult for one not acquainted with the spot to discover.

Stimulated by the rewards offered, or by a desire to gain the plaudits that the consummation of the act would secure, as well as probable promotion, a young and daring English officer, Captain Boyd, then in Canada, but unattached, undertook the project of effecting the capture of Johnson, and proceeded in a cautious and systematic manner that promised success, if that was possible.

Enlisting half a score of trusty men, to but a couple of whom, however, he intrusted the secret of his mission, he quietly started out upon a cruise among the islands in a yacht, under the guise of a sportsman. This gave him sufficient excuse for going well armed. Fortune at length rewarded the perseverance of Captain Boyd; and the secret of the outlaw's retreat was disclosed to him, as is believed, by one of Johnson's band, to whom a few gold pieces proved a stronger incentive than the oath of fidelity given to his leader. He also became cognizant of the fact that the disturber of the peace was sojourning at the cave, accompanied by but half a dozen followers; and by watching the opportunity Captain Boyd was enabled not only to surprise him when there was but a single follower with him, but to effect an entrance to the cavern unopposed, backed by his men, who with presented rifles covered the two inmates.

The insurgent leader could not but manifest some trepidation at first at this very unexpected intrusion, but almost at once recovered his presence of mind, and in a firm voice demanded, —

"Who are you? What means this?"

"I am Captain Boyd, of the English Army, and you are my prisoner!" was the prompt reply.

"Well, Captain, I will not dispute you," returned Johnson, coolly; "but come in, and we will talk the matter over."

As he spoke, he pointed to a seat upon a keg at one side of the cavern, which apartment was of about ten feet in width by something less than forty in length.

The captain accepted the proffered seat, and at a glance surveyed the strange room. The view that it presented was in keeping with the character and pursuits of those whose home it was. Rifles, powder-flasks, and bullet-pouches adorned the walls; at the further end were couches formed of branches of evergreens covered with blankets; at one side was a rude fireplace, the smoke from which found its way upward through a crevice in the rocks above, while the place was lighted by day by the aperture of a hollow tree-trunk sunk through the roof so skilfully that upon the outside it appeared to have grown there.

The others remained at the entrance, with rifles held ready to answer any possible demonstration on the part of the two prisoners.

"It is a rule," resumed Johnson, as he took a bottle from a shelf in the rock, "that all persons who visit Fort Wallace shall partake of its hospitalities. We are plain people here, and have no use for the luxuries of life, among which we rank glasses; so be kind enough to partake from the bottle."

The captain, astonished at and admiring the coolness of his captive, courteously accepted it, and placed it to his lips; but, fearful of some ruse, permitted none of the drink to pass them.

"*Your friends*," said Johnson, "will they not partake?"

"No, thanks," returned the captain, smiling involuntarily; "not upon this occasion!"

"We have a little business to transact, and I suppose that you are impatient, and that the subject is open for remark. To commence, what do you wish of me?"

"To accompany me at once."

"To what place, permit me to inquire?" and as he asked this he seated himself upon the head of a barrel opposite to the captain.

"To whatever place we may choose to convey you."

"To Kingston, perhaps?"

"Quite likely."

The captive appeared to reflect for a moment; then he walked toward the fireplace and took from one of his pockets a pipe.

"No objections to my smoking, I suppose?" he inquired.

"None at all."

The outlaw calmly proceeded to fill the pipe; then he took from the embers a large coal and placed it upon it, and, returning to his seat upon the barrel, proceeded to give a couple of invigorating whiffs.

"Come," spoke the Captain, "I cannot delay longer; you must come at once."

Johnson calmly removed the pipe from his lips and held it in his hand.

"I object to accompanying you to Kingston," he said. "This barrel," he continued, with a meaning glance, as he observed the expression of surprise upon the countenance of the other, and removed one of the boards of the lid, "contains powder; and this," as he held the pipe over it, "is a coal! Shall we make the journey?"

Brave as he was, it is feared that the adventurous captain, as he quickly comprehended the situation, paled a little, while his followers made a rapid movement toward the entrance of the cavern, and sought safety in flight, save a couple, more valiant than the rest, who remained at the door to keep Johnson and his single follower covered with their pieces.

A pause succeeded,—an unpleasant one for all, since a spark from the coal, or the coal itself, was momentarily liable to fall into the barrel of powder and usher them into eternity without further warning.

Johnson was the first to speak. "You should have known, Captain," he said, "that William Johnson could never be taken alive; now we can treat on equal terms,—a life for a life, if you so decide!"

"I confess myself beaten," commenced the captain, rising as he spoke.

"Keep your seat!" thundered Johnson, handling the pipe menacingly.

The captain resumed his place upon the keg.

"Now I will listen to you," said the outlaw.

"I was about to say that I was willing to confess myself beaten, and propose that we call this a draw,—we depart, and you remain in peace."

"That is satisfactory," rejoined the other; "but hold a moment—Here, Sam," addressing his follower, who stood a few yards off, "hand me a coal from the fire."

The man silently obeyed. Johnson received it, while the others watched him

"KEEP YOUR SEAT!"

apprehensively, and placed it upon the head of the barrel, a few inches from the powder, where it gleamed with vindictive brightness. "The pipe is in danger of going out," he said, in explanation, "and I wish to keep another in readiness. Now, to continue, my terms are that you not only depart in peace, but that you give me your word of honor that you will not again attempt to molest me in any manner unless you should be called upon to do so in self-defence, — that you will not disclose the secret of this retreat to any one, and that you will require the same pledge from each and all of your men."

"I agree to them," said the Captain, promptly.

"And give me your oath upon it?" said Johnson.

"I do, upon the honor of an officer of the English army; and now I suppose that we may depart?"

The captain, rising, left the cavern as soon as consistent with official dignity, preceded by the two men who had remained at the entrance. The remainder of the party were found a short distance away, and, re-entering their boat, they took speedy departure.

They were quickly followed from the cave by Johnson and his follower, rifles in hand, who, somewhat distrustful in regard to the good faith of their late captors, hurried to a spot on the island whence such of their companions as were in the vicinity could be summoned by signal to hasten at once to the rendezvous.

The signal had hardly been displayed, and the boat of Captain Boyd had not disappeared behind the nearest island, when there was heard a loud explosion. The cavern was blown up.

Louis Robinson followed this curious provincial story by Chapin with a narrative that received close attention.

"The story that I have to offer," he said, "would seem much like an attempt to create a female Robinson Crusoe, were it not true. But, strange as they may seem, all the incidents are true."

THE LEGEND OF MARGUERITE AND THE ISLE OF DEMONS.

Belle Isle and the Isle of Demons! The old French voyagers and explorers welcomed the one and shunned the other. Among the most thrilling tales told in the halls of French noblemen was that of the Isle of the Devils, situated in the tossing sea on the north of the New-Found-Land.

The island lay as it were at the portal of the unknown world, — a world of stupendous boundaries and resources, of red nations and plumed chiefs, of cloud-swept mountains and mighty water-courses. In the bosom of almost limitless forests were sequestered clans. In the south were lands of perpetual summer, festive peoples, and palaces of gold.

The shores of Labrador and of Anticosti were dark and gloomy, even in midsummer. Strange wild birds made their nests there. The old explorers

THE ISLE OF DEMONS.

horns, and arms having wings, seems to have been *howling*. These howlings were thought to fill all the near regions of the seas.

"True it is," says an old adventurer, — "and I myself have heard it, not from one, but from a great number of sailors and pilots with whom I have made voyages, — that when they passed this way they heard in the air, on the tops of the masts and about them, a great clamor of voices, like a crowd in a market-place. Then they knew that the Isle of Demons was not far away."

The same sounds, it is said, may be heard near the island to-day ; but the most superstitious sailor would not think of attributing them to anything but the peculiar winds and currents of the air. The wildness of the sea and the mournfulness of the winds have not changed ; but the world has grown in intelligence, and in the light of science the demons, like the griffins, have disappeared from the imaginations of the toilers around the Banks.

There was a certain voyager, a nobleman of Picardy, known in history as Sieur de Roberval. He was made a viceroy of New France about the year 1542. He might as well have been made viceroy of the air or the sea ; but his titles in this new capacity surpassed in pompous words those of any nobleman in France. He was Lord of Norembega, Lieutenant-General of Canada, and Viceroy of Canada, Hochelaga, Saguenay, Newfoundland, Labrador, and other places of equal space on paper. He was a man of hard heart ; the best place for him would have been on the desolate Isle of Demons, which came at last to bear his name.

He sailed out of the sunny harbor of Rochelle, in April, 1642, having three ships and two hundred colonists, bound for the St. Lawrence. In June he entered the harbor of St. John.

Among the passengers was a niece of Roberval, a young lady of wonderful beauty, who was called Marguerite. She had been loved, in the bright province whence she came, by a gentleman who was ill-regarded by Roberval. When this gentleman found that her uncle was resolved to take her to the new world, he also joined the expedition, determined like a true lover to share the perils, fortunes, and fate of the lovely Marguerite.

Out of the Bay of Biscay, on their way to the wonderful regions of the west, the lovers renewed their interviews, and seemed to have little thought or care but for each other's society. Roberval discovered the renewed affection with anger.

"I will leave you, Marguerite," he said, "to die on the Isle of Demons."

"And I will share your fate," whispered her lover in her ear.

The attachment continued. The ship was moving north toward the haunted isle. Winds began to whistle about the tops of the masts, and the sounds were believed to be evil spirits' voices. Marguerite believed the superstition, and she knew the fate that awaited her, and began to pray to the Virgin, who she thought would espouse her cause and shield her from the dark spirits of the air.

The ship on which were Roberval and Marguerite drew near the wild island one summer day. Roberval cast anchor, and compelled Marguerite to land, giving her, as a parting portion, a certain amount of arms and provisions and an old Norman nurse for an attendant.

Roberval had resolved to sail away in the fogs and shadows, and to take with him Marguerite's lover for future revenges. He was delighting in his power over the crushed Marguerite, as she stood weeping on the windy shore, when a man leaped overboard, and was lost in the foaming surf. He rose again, at a point near the shore. The sailors and emigrants looked upon the sea and rocks in dumb astonishment. The fugitive reached the shore and joined Marguerite, and the three fled into the piny forests whence no Frenchman or Indian would have dared to pursue them. The fugitive was the lover of Marguerite.

The exiles built them a cabin overlooking the restless sea. They heard the north winds in the pine tops at night, and thought them the voices of demons. When the storms were gathering the voices were fearful. Then the beautiful Marguerite would kneel and pray to the Virgin.

Marguerite's faith in the Virgin was her comfort now, and that of her lover and companion. When the demons came to destroy them, as the exiles fancied they often did as they heard the winds and the howlings of beasts of prey, Marguerite looked upward to the Virgin, and thought she saw a white hand stretch out above her. Then all was peace.

The exiles gathered eggs and berries in summer, and nuts in autumn. The woods were filled with game, and the sea with fish; and they laid in a good supply of food for the winter.

The winter came. They had watched the sea for a sail, but none had appeared. Strange gaunt-looking animals began to prowl about the cabin, such as they had never seen in France. They believed them to be demons.

When the howlings of these animals became fearful at night, Marguerite would pray, and she would see the white hand; and then the exiles would rest in peace and consolation.

So Marguerite's prayers, as she believed, dropped the white hand of the Virgin like a heavenly lily, and the heaven of her heart shone serenely over the dark and demon-haunted islands and seas.

Winter vanished. The soft spring came. The June roses bloomed. A child was born to Marguerite. They were four now, — five, if one could believe Marguerite's own narrative of the presence of the Virgin.

The hardships of the winter had broken the health of the follower of her strange fortunes, and he did not have that faith in the white hand that made Marguerite so strong and hopeful. He grew thin, and, consumed by fevers, died in the summer time, craving life for the sake of the mother and child.

The old Norman nurse and Marguerite made his grave where they could watch it and guard it from the beasts and demons. The burial was such as has seldom been seen, — two women and the infant stood above the coffinless body, and the old nurse wrung her hands, and the mother repeated the ancient prayers. The beasts prowled around the cabin, the mysterious voices were heard in the air ; but Marguerite still trusted and prayed, and looked hopefully out on the empty sea, and still dreamed that she saw the white hand of the Virgin.

The child died. The grave was made beside the father's. The mourners were two.

The old Norman nurse died. There was but one to dig the grave and one mourner now.

Marguerite was alone — alone, as she believed, with the demons. But as often as they came, she prayed, and as often the fancied white hand appeared.

Bears prowled around the cabin and tried to enter. She thought them monsters. She says that she killed three that were white.

She watched the three graves and the helpless sea. She again saw the snows melt, and the birds return from the suns of the south.

One day she saw afar a speck on the water. It was the boat of some fishermen. She kindled fires and fed them. The boatmen saw them, and came to the island. They carried Marguerite away.

She returned to France and told her melancholy story to her courtly friends, who welcomed her back. She died in peace, led to Paradise, as she doubtless believed, by the white hand in which she had trusted in her forest cabin.

What was the fate of Roberval ?

The Canadian winter followed him. With it came famine to the colony, then pestilence. But misfortunes and disasters only served to harden his heart. He governed with an iron hand. He hung six men in one day ; the whipping-post was kept in constant use ; he banished some who displeased him to desolate islands ; others he put in fetters. The colony came to speedy ruin. Roberval returned to France overwhelmed with his calamities, even before poor Marguerite found her way back over the sea.

Still he retained the favor of the Court.

Years passed. One night there was a murder near the Church of the Innocents in the heart of Paris. The tragedy sent a thrill of excitement through the streets. The dying victim saw no white hand in the gathering shadows of death. There was a red hand in his dreams ; he must have felt the end was but the fruit of his own deeds, the result of his own example and conduct, whatever may have been the immediate cause or whoever may have struck the blow. It was Roberval.

Other stories were told by members of the Club ; but we have not space for them here.

The exercises were closed by an original poem, written by Louis Robinson and spoken by Charlie Noble. Each verse ended with a chorus that was rather mixed in idioms, but put every one in good humor.

OUR BROTHER LANDS.

I stood beside the Rhine.
  The night was falling dark ;
The student clubs were singing
  In the gardens and the park.
Then said the young Bavarians.
  "Join our chorus if you can."
But I could only answer them,
  "Ich bin Américan."
    "Ich bin Américan ?
      Bravo America !
    It is our brother land,
      Bravo America !
    She 's the country of the free.
      The friend of every man ;
    Here 's a heart and hand for thee,
      Er ist Américan ! "

I saw the snowy Alps
  By sunset bridges spanned,
And over fair Lucerne
  Night stretched her jewelled hand.
"Sing with us the Edelweiss ; "
  And the Alpine song began.
But I could only answer them,
  "Je suis Américan."
    "Je suis Américan ?
      Viva America !
    It is our brother land.
      Viva America !
    She 's the country of the free.
      The friend of every man ;
    Here 's a heart and hand for thee,
      Il est Américan."

In Italy's deep lakes
  We dipped our silvered oars,
And cleft the shadowy peaks
  That were glassed from Como's shores.

"Sing for us a barcarole,"
  Said the boatmen on the way.
"Sono Americáno,"
  Was all that I could say.
    "Sono Americáno?"
      Viva America!
    It is our brother land,
      Viva America!
    She's the country of the free,
      The friend of every man;
    Here's a heart and hand for thee,
      Lui Americán!"

From terraces of Basle
  I gazed o'er Jura's plain;
They were singing the old ballads
  Of Alsace and Lorraine.
Then said the gay Alsatians,
  "Sing for freedom, if you can.'
But I could only say again,
  "Je suis Americán."
    "Je suis Americán?
      Viva America!
    It is our brother land,
      Viva America!
    She's the country of the free,
      The friend of every man;
    Here's a heart and hand for thee,
      Il est Americán."

Above Granada's towers
  High rose the sun of night;
And mid the evening's splendor
  They danced to music light.
They called me to the merry throng;
  I sadly turned away.
"Yo soy Americáno?"
  Was all that I could say.
    "Yo soy Americáno?
      Viva America!
    It is our brother land,
      Viva America!
    She's the country of the free,
      The friend of every man;
    Here's a heart and hand for thee,
      Il es Americán!"

He may wander by the Rhine,
  He may wander by the Rhine,
In the old and storied lands
  Of Alp or Apennine;
But wherever be his way,
  Royal greetings wait the man
Whose honest lips can say,
  "I am Americán."
    Il est Americán,
      Viva America!
    Er ist Americán,
      Bravo America!
    Brother hearts and brother hands
      Shall welcome him afar;
    For all lands are the brother lands
      Of our own America.

CHAPTER IV.

CARDINAL RICHELIEU'S DREAM OF NEW FRANCE.

CHAMPLAIN'S STORY OF HIS SURPRISE OF FATHER JOSEPH ON THE SHORES OF
LAKE HURON.

 HE study of the early history of Canada proved to the Class a romance, as Master Lewis had predicted. The teacher added the works of Schoolcraft to the books already mentioned that he had desired the class to read.

"Schoolcraft," he said, "will give you a view of the part that the Indians played in this threefold drama of history."

At one of the recitations the teacher unexpectedly brought before the students a very interesting and dramatic figure of history.

"Henry IV.," he said, "married for his second wife Mary de' Medici. His son, Louis XIII., a mere lad, succeeded him, with Mary de' Medici as regent. Mary was a Florentine, and she had brought from Florence, at the time of her marriage, her most intimate friends, Concino Concini, and his wife, Leonora Galigaï. The latter were vulgar, ambitious people, without personal worth, brilliant, magnetic, emotional, vain.

"Strange were the days of the old kings, and we cannot wonder that there were revolutions. Here we find the great French nation governed by an Italian woman, and herself influenced in matters of state by her own servants; for such her Italian favorites were. Leonora Galigaï was the daughter of an old Italian nurse; and the

CONCINI, LEONORA GALIGAÏ, AND MARY DE' MEDICI.

strange circumstances I have given put under her influence the whole
French nation.

"The husband of Leonora turned his position at Court to his
own private profit, and became very rich. He purchased for himself
the Marquisate of Ancre; and Mary made him Marshal of France.
Think of it, — a Florentine adventurer made Marshal of France
because he had married a favorite servant of an Italian wife of a
king!

"'I have learned to know the world,' he said. 'When I came to
France, I was not worth a sou, and I owed eight thousand crowns.
My marriage and the queen's favor have given me office and honor.'

"This pompous man, Marshal d'Ancre, aspired to be the guardian
of the boy king, Louis XIII.

"Louis had one intimate friend, Albert de Luynes, an expert in
the training of birds for hunting. The young king made him his
falconer.

"One day the king and Marshal d'Ancre were playing at billiards
together.

"'I hope your Majesty will allow me to wear my hat,' said the
proud marshal, with a cool indifference to the etiquette of the Court,
which all noblemen observed.

"The young king did not object; but Albert de Luynes was
offended at the Italian's insolence. He probably set on foot a plot
for the marshal's assassination.

"It became known at Court that the young king desired to be free
from the Florentine's influence.

"One day an army officer of rank came to the king, and said, —

"'You are now King of France. Marshal d'Ancre is dead.'

"But amid weak, cruel, degrading scenes like these, a young man
was rising like a giant who was to reduce the king and the regent
to virtual slavery to his own will, who was to govern France for
twenty years and influence all the powers of Europe. He was to

be in peace what Napoleon afterwards was in war. His career serves to show how genius climbs to a throne over the thrones of kings. This man, nothing but a monk, gained the mastery not only of France and the French provinces, but of nearly all Europe, by an all-powerful will and the mere force of genius for governing.

"Let us look at his first advent into political life.

"At the convocation of the states-general in 1614, there appeared among the delegates a young bishop, Armand de Richelieu. He was born in 1585, and was then twenty-eight years old. He had already won the admiration of the Pope by a brilliant Latin oration in Rome. He was consecrated Bishop at Rome.

"He was a worldly prelate, fond of pomp and power. He exhibited a very strange spirit for a minister of Christ on entering upon his duties as bishop in an humble see.

"'I should very much like to make more *show*,' he wrote to one of his fair friends; 'but what can I do? No house, no carriage, I must borrow a coach, horses, and a *coachman*, in order to arrive at Lucon with a decent turn-out.'

"We may hope that when he did arrive at his diocese with his borrowed coachman, the people placed a true value upon the spectacle.

"He was able to make more show after his election to the states-general. He here began to exercise those arts of diplomacy that at last made him the master of kings.

"He had magnetic eloquence. His tongue was able to charm the great, and he sought the audience of nobles. He began to champion the idea that prelates were not sufficiently recognized by sovereigns, nor duly consulted in state councils.

"But at the same time and in the same breath he paid a glowing tribute to the great wisdom of the young king in intrusting the affairs of state to his mother. He accomplished three things at one stroke by this brilliant address, — he pleased the young king; he

LOUIS XIII. AND ALBERT DE LUYNES.

delighted the queen mother; and he led Mary, agreeing that prelates should be more consulted in affairs of state, to invite *him* to take up his residence at Court as her almoner. The foolish woman, who had not yet learned that a flatterer never has a true heart or purpose, little dreamed what she was doing. You shall be told how it ended at last.

"The new almoner made his first intimacy at Court with the pompous Marshal d'Ancre, then the favorite of the queen-regnant. When the marshal was assassinated, the good bishop made his next intimacy with the young king's favorite, Albert de Luynes, who had brought about the marshal's overthrow and death. He had received from the marshal the office of Secretary of State and of War for Foreign Affairs; but this was nothing, now the marshal was no more.

"After the death of her Italian favorite, Mary de' Medici retired to Blois. Richelieu asked the young king's leave to follow her there.

"'I can make myself,' he said, 'more useful to your Majesty there than in any other position.'

"The king knew this to be true. Richelieu would use his influence over Mary in his behalf. He was sent to Blois.

"It would take a volume to describe all the arts by which this prelate of soaring ambition gained complete mastery over the mind of the young king. But this he accomplished in the end, and, driving Mary into exile, became the virtual sovereign of France.

"Louis XIII. was a weak king. He associated with his falconer, who profited every way that he could by the association. The king said to him one day, —

"'I never saw one person with so many relatives. They come to the Court in ship-loads, and not one of them has a silk dress.'

"Affairs of state he left wholly to Richelieu. Listless and irresolute, he did not feel that a born king should be burdened with the cares of state-craft. What the cardinal advised, he did.

"One or two stories of the ambitious cardinal will serve to show how he retained the power that he so craftily obtained.

"Mary de' Medici, finding that Richelieu's influence over the king had supplanted her own, resolved, in 1630, to secure the cardinal's dismissal from affairs of state, by awakening the king's jealousy and inciting him to a more ambitious use of the royal power. She followed her son wherever he went, and ceased not to denounce the ambition of the cardinal.

"Richelieu began to suspect that he was distrusted by Mary, and to fear that a conspiracy against him would grow out of the great intimacy that had been renewed between the royal mother and her weak son.

"The king and Mary were at Luxembourg, a palace which Mary had just finished and furnished. It was November 12. The cardinal was supposed to be at the capital attending to a crisis of affairs growing out of difficulties in Italy.

"There appeared suddenly, at the gates of the new palace, a tall dark man. He entered. He went to the door of the council chamber and knocked. No one answered. He knocked at the door of the cabinet, but still met with no response.

"He pushed his way into the private chapel.

"Mary and the king were there.

"As soon as Mary beheld the cardinal her heart sunk within her.

"'Here he is,' said the shallow king, in a tone of despair.

"'You were talking of *me*,' said the cardinal to Mary, as though such an act would be treason.

"Mary cowered before the piercing eyes and the tall dark form.

"'I am sure you were talking of me.'

"'We were not,' said Mary.

"The cardinal, who seldom failed to worm out a secret, assumed his clerical dignity, and said,—

"'Confess it.'

MURDER OF MARSHAL D'ANCRE.

"His manner was resolute.

"'Yes,' said Mary, weakly.

"The confession was the turning-point of her destiny.

"'I will never see the cardinal again,' she said after the confession, 'nor any of his relatives and friends. He shall be dismissed.'

"The cardinal had made a like resolution in regard to his former benefactress.

"After this surprise the enemies of the cardinal flocked to the Luxembourg. Louis XIII. considered the political situation. The affairs of state were so in the hands of the cardinal, and all the public departments were so under his control, that he dared not dismiss him.

"He sent for the cardinal. During the interview the latter asserted his terrible power, and gained a complete mastery over the mind of the king. The day of the conference became famous as Dupe's Day. As the result, Mary de' Medici fled from France; and the ambitious woman never saw her son again. Her life was blighted from the moment the dark form of the cardinal entered the palace. She died, wretched and poor, at Cologne.

"Twelve years afterwards, another conspiracy was set on foot against the cardinal. Among the favorites of Louis was Cinq-Mars, whom he had made his grand-equerry. He was brilliant, witty, handsome, and independent. The weak king formed an attachment for him, — an affection that became silly and capricious. Louis used to confide to the cardinal the secrets of this friendship. Cinq-Mars seems at least to have had a certain amount of self-respect, and often refused to yield to the tempers of the king.

"'I am very sorry,' wrote the king to Richelieu, 'to trouble you with the ill feelings of M. le Grand. I upbraided him, but he answered that he could not change. I said that, considering his obligations to me, he ought not to address me in that manner. He answered that he did not want my kindness, that he could do very well without it, and that he would be quite as content to be Cinq-Mars as M. le Grand.'

"This fascinating nobleman did his best to make the king suspicious of the influence of the cardinal. He probably arranged a plot for the cardinal's destruction, and hoped to profit by his overthrow. The king gave a ready ear to his favorite, and is believed at first to have favored the plot.

"But if he did, his thoughts reacted as before. In a few days the Court was astonished at the intelligence that the king had ordered the arrest of Cinq-Mars, Grand Equerry of France.

"Shortly after the king wrote to Richelieu,—

"'I love you more than ever. We have been too long together ever to be separated; and I wish everybody to understand it."

"When he was accused of being false to Cinq-Mars, he said,—

"'I listened, and seemed to favor his plans in order to find out all that was in his wicked heart.'

"The friendship of intellect is more powerful than that of passion, as Cinq-Mars saw as he marched to his death.

"Richelieu is termed, in the history and philosophy of politics, an Absolutist. By the term is meant an advocate of the absolute power of the king. He believed that kings were the divinely appointed agents of government. It was his aim to make the power of the French king absolute. As a result of his policy to this end, Louis XIV. was able to say, 'I am the State,' and Louis XV. was called 'France.'

"The government during the great reign of Henry IV. *Henri Quatre*, as he was called — was greatly influenced by the nobles and the people. The Edict of Nantes, giving all men liberty of worship, was an advance toward republicanism. It was the aim of Richelieu to change this policy, to crush out this growing freedom.

"You have heard much about the policy and statesmanship of Richelieu. What was it?

LOUIS XIII

"There were parliaments in the provinces of France. These made local laws, much like our legislatures. It was the policy of Richelieu to take from these their independent power.

"There was feudalism in France, — lords who were supreme rulers of vast estates. It was the policy of Richelieu to crush these feudal rivals of the throne.

"There was a party in France called the Huguenots. They were Protestant Calvinists, and had become a political power. Richelieu did not meddle with freedom of worship. He has been called the Huguenot Cardinal. But he believed that the Huguenots, as a political power, were dangerous to the throne. He determined to crush the party as well as the parliaments, and the exercise of independent power by feudal lords.

"Thus, to make the king *absolute* was the one idea of Richelieu.

"Louis XIII. knew the value of such a minister. Louis loved the reputation of being a powerful ruler. To Richelieu he sacrificed his mother and friends. To him he surrendered the government wholly; and Richelieu returned him a puissant throne and a splendid name among the courts of the age.

"It was night at Fontainebleau. The old château of France had grown in splendor for a hundred years. It was a forest palace now, — a favorite resort of the king, nobles, and ministers of state. In the moonlight nights gayly lighted boats drifted by it, and troubadours played under its windows.

"The cardinal was at Fontainebleau. The Court and nobles were there. Astrals blazed in the halls, and the nobles were making merry in the banquet room and council chamber.

"'We have a new arrival,' said a courtier to the cardinal.

"'Who?'

"'The knight-errant, is he not? or only an adventurer? Samuel de Champlain, the old story-teller of the Court of Henri Quatre.'

"'Ask him in,' said Richelieu.

"In a few minutes the old voyager on the St. Lawrence and the explorer of the mighty lake that is to eternally bear his name appeared, and was courteously received by the cardinal and nobles.

"The names of Champlain and Richelieu are linked in fame. The river Richelieu connects the great lake with the St. Lawrence.

"The old voyager was again asked to relate some new episode of his romantic adventures. This he did somewhat as follows: —

PLANTING THE CROSS IN NEW LANDS.

"May it please your Eminence, I will speak of my recent adventures in those regions that seem to have no boundaries or limits, that lie in the marvellous empire of the West. The great fresh-water sea of the Hurons is there; and it has been my privilege to plant there the flag of the Fleur-de-lis beside the Cross. It will be a glorious day for France when she shall people this wonderful empire and make tributary its numberless tribes, and when the Fleur-de-lis shall float over every harbor and the Cross shall shine over every town. Wider than Europe will be the domain. The glory of the new empire will rival the old.

CINQ-MARS AND DE THOU GOING TO EXECUTION.

JESUIT MISSIONARY ADDRESSING THE INDIANS.

"'You all remember my departure for the West with the Recollets, those noble champions of the Cross. We were blessed by his

Holiness, the Pope, and honored by our most gracious king. The bishops, cardinals, and nobles loaded us with favors, with vestments for our altars and candles for our shrines.

"'Father Joseph le Charon accepted as his mission field the country of the Hurons. He had no sooner arrived at Quebec than he became impatient to go to his field in the wilderness.

"'In the fall a great multitude of Indians gather at Montreal for trade. The Huron chiefs come there.

"'Thither hurried Father Joseph, hoping to gain a knowledge of the language of the Hurons, and to learn much in regard to the regions of the great inland seas.

"'"I shall winter among the Indians," said he.

"'I spoke to him of the hardships and perils of such a life.

"'"What," he said, "are privations to me, who have devoted my life to poverty and who have no ambition but to serve God?"

"'I left him among the traders, and promised to return.

"'When I went back to Montreal, the Indians were gone to the country of the great seas, and Father Joseph had gone with them.

"'I wished to see the country of the Hurons. I was told that it was a land of majestic lakes and calm and beautiful seas. The river Ottawa led to it. I resolved to follow Father Joseph, and to surprise him in his forest home.

"'It was summer. I launched my canoe on the Ottawa. I paddled along under the shadows of lofty mountains. The stream was calm; the days were resplendent, and the forest the most noble I ever beheld. Ten Indians, a companion, and an interpreter went with me.

"'I came at last in sight of the great inland ocean. It was calm, noble, and beautiful. There is no scene like it in France. "Glorious," we called it, and so it is, — the ocean of the Hurons, far, far in the West.

"'The Indians had heard of Father Joseph. They consented to conduct me to his mission. I longed to see the true Cross towering

CASTLE OF FONTAINEBLEAU.

over the blue sea, and to plant beside it the Lilies of France. We hurried on.

"'The land was one of beauty and abundance. In the openings of the great forest were maize fields, over which the glowing sun poured its splendors and the lake winds blew. Here and there were patches of pumpkins, and gardens of sunflowers.

"'We came to Otonacha, where were the lodges of the mighty nation. I was received as a champion of the tribe, and in the great lodge of the place I was entertained by a feast at which were assembled the chief men, who presented a scene of barbaric luxury and splendor.

"'I was escorted in a kind of triumphal procession to Carhagonha. It was the fortress of the Hurons. It consisted of a triple palisade some thirty-five feet high, where dwelt the warriors and where were stored their arms and resources of war. The fortress swarmed with gayly plumed defenders. Here again I was received as a champion. Feast after feast was spread for me; rude instruments of music sounded, and there were fantastic dances under the August moon.

"'In the midst of the festivities I saw a band of Indians approaching the place in grave and stately demeanor. They were followed by a tall form in a dark robe. Behind him were a band of men whom I knew to be Europeans.

"'As the august company came into a nearer view, the dark-robed man hurried forward. He seemed chanting a *Te Deum*, and to be filled with inexpressible joy. The band of Indians divided, and the tall man rushed into my arms.

"'"Father Joseph," I said, "defender of the Cross, Providence has sent me hither!"

"'"Champlain, defender of the Faith and of the Lilies of France, peace be unto you, and the blessings of the Queen of Heaven attend you! Let us return thanks! I have planted the Cross here in the wilderness. Let us go to the forest sanctuary!"

"'" I will go, Father Joseph, and I will again set the Lilies of France beside the Cross."

"' It was August 12th, — a dreamy day, as though heaven had let down a curtain of gold around the forest, and canopied the regions with purple. Beyond were the fresh seas, which the chiefs said had no limits, but were linked one to another by foaming rivers and straits.

"' Father Joseph was arrayed in the vestments that had been given him by the bishops and nobles of Paris, who could never have imagined that he would wear them on an occasion like this. Behind him were our twelve brothers of the Cross who had followed his fortunes from Montreal, and Etienne Brule, the interpreter.

"' The chapel was simple, but it was adorned with the precious emblems of the faith. It was filled with dusky forms. My heart glowed as I beheld these children of the forest sign themselves with the Cross, and bow before the emblem of the Light of the World that shone upon the altar.

"' We sung the *Te Deum Laudamus*. Then at my order a volley of guns proclaimed the triumph of the faith, and I planted the flag beside the Cross.

> '" Ye heroes of the Cross, advance !
> O mystery of the Cross, shine forth !"''

" The Court listened to the narrative with joy and wonder. Even the cold cardinal was moved. If statecraft had not absorbed him, a missionary spirit would have fired his soul. He was silent when the story ended. He had begun to dream. The cardinal's day-dreams always came true. His dream was of a New France, a France beyond the sea.

" The French Protestants or Huguenots made Rochelle the head-quarters of their party. Rochelle was a lovely city by the sea, surrounded by powerful fortifications. Its harbor was filled with ships.

" It was a favorite resort of the English, and of Protestant traders. It was for a long period under English rule, being a part of the wedding dowry of Eleanor of Aquitaine, on her marriage with Henry II. Richelieu determined to crush the Huguenot power as one of the enemies of the throne, and he laid siege to Rochelle.

THE KING AND RICHELIEU AT LA ROCHELLE.

" ' The Huguenot party,' said the cardinal, ' has for a hundred years divided the kingdom. Demolish her fortifications. Let no vessel of war enter her harbor from abroad.'

" The order was carried out. But the spirit of the Huguenots was unchanged. Then came the siege, one of the most memorable in history.

" John Guiton, a hero with the iron will of a martyr, was made mayor of the lovely and imperilled city.

" ' I accept the honor,' he said to the Rochellese ; ' but,' he added, throwing a poniard upon the table, — ' but on the condition that yonder weapon shall pierce the heart of him who dares speak of surrender.'

"The king accompanied the cardinal to Rochelle, and watched with him the progress of the siege. Months passed. The suffering in the place became fearful. England attempted to help her Protestant friends, and sent a fleet to their assistance; but the expedition was defeated. Famine filled the city with corpses. The soldiers

THE KING AND THE CARDINAL.

themselves became almost fleshless. It was a dead city. There were corpses in the chambers, the houses, the streets. The city was vanquished at last by the famine, and then surrendered to Richelieu.

"The king and Richelieu triumphantly entered the gates and gazed upon the work that they had wrought.

"The policy of Richelieu was again omnipotent; the Protestant party, as a political power in France, was dead.

"Richelieu now dreamed of making Europe bend to his will in the name of the King of France. His dream came true.

JOHN GUITON'S OATH.

"But his restless brain was haunted by the more romantic dream of the empire of the West. He pondered over the tales of Champlain. Might not the glories of France be re-mapped in the New World? Might there not arise a new France in the empires of the Iroquois, Algonquins, and Hurons, that would fill the treasury with gold and restore to the throne the puissance of Charlemagne?

"All Europe had been thrilled with the exploits of the mariners of the West.

"The Cabots had followed Columbus; Ponce de Leon, the Cabots. The former had beheld the colossal shores of the North, and the latter the almost paradisaic beauty of the South. In 1513 Balboa had looked upon the Pacific. The conquests of Cortez had dazzled Spain. Then followed the wonderful achievements of Verrazano, Narvaez, Cartier, De Soto, Cabrillo. Espejo had founded Santa Fé, and De Monts had dwelt amid the rugged scenes of Nova Scotia.

"Now came Champlain, with his tales of inland oceans and of nations of which no mind had conceived.

"Richelieu dreamed again. His powerful mind was the master of France; he aspired to the mastery of the courts of Europe. The way seemed clear to this great ambition. But the courts of Europe did not fill his dream.

"In his palace hung the rude maps of the mariners of the West. He beheld the great empire of the West in a vision. Its hills were crowned with crosses; over its harbors glimmered the emblem of the faith, and beside every cross flowered the Lilies of France.

"Another stroke of policy: He suppressed the ancient office of Admiral of France.

"Another: He made himself the Grand Master and Superintendent of Navigation and Commerce.

"Another: He formed a trading company of a hundred men. He called it the "Company of New France;" and the most conspicuous man of these hundred associates was Samuel de Champlain.

"New France! It was a splendid dream. Would that all the dreams which he had dreamed at the Louvre, the Tuileries, and at Fontainebleau had been as glorious!

"My story is a picture. I hope you will follow the fulfilment of Richelieu's dream."

CHAPTER V.

E must make up a programme that will commend itself to Master Lewis," said Charlie Noble to the Musical Society. "I have the impression that our vocal gifts are not the most remarkable; so we must select pieces that have interest in themselves."

"It will not do to include 'The Red, White, and Blue' with the words that I wrote for the Club," said Charlie Leland.

" Why ? "

" If we should ever repeat the concert in the Provinces, the English would not like that."

" I do not think so. The English stand by their own flag and country, and sing lustily, ' Rule, Britannia ; ' and they respect the same feeling among people of other nations. Yes ; we must include that."

" But they might hiss you."

" Then I would sing them the song of the ' Fine Old English Gentleman ' who had better manners."

" Or throw beans at you."

" I would then sing them ' The Sword of Bunker Hill,' and remind them that our fathers did not throw beans at their grandfathers in those days. But I am not afraid of any trouble of that kind. An Englishman likes pluck, and respects it. Americans respect an

English 'middy,' and the whole-souled Englishman will respect a true-hearted American boy."

"Let us take for our first piece ' Oh, my America!'" said Charlie. "That song includes the whole country, and admits of the emotional tone."

"Capital," said Noble.

" The Hampton singers' songs were popular in the Provinces; why could we not include some of the Indian songs that were popular years ago," asked Charlie Leland, — "such as Mrs. Hunter's Indian's Death-Song, ' The sun sets at night and the stars shun the day,' and ' When shall we three meet again ? ' composed by an Indian graduate of Dartmouth College, or the queer old mission song, ' In de dark wood, no Injun nigh ' ? "

"That is a good idea," said Noble. " I am sure that the last song you name would be interesting. I once heard my grandfather sing it. Do you recall the words ? "

" A part of them : —

> " ' In de dark wood, no Injun nigh,
> Den me look heben, send up cry,
>   Upon my knees so low.
> God hear poor Injun in de wood ;
> Den me lub God, an' dat be good,
>   De priest, he tell me so.
>
> " ' Den God, He say, " Poor Injun, come ;
> Me goin' to take poor Injun home,
>   Where he may lib in heben."
> Den Injun he wing up an' fly,
> An' tell de angels 'bove de sky
>   How he hab been forgiben.
>
> " ' When me be old, me head be gray,
> He neber lebe me, — so He say, —
>   He wid me till me die,
> Den take me up to shiny place,
> See red man, white man, black man face ;
>   All happy den on high.'"

" That ought to be as entertaining as ' Mary and Martha have just gone along,' " said Noble. " We must learn some of the best of the old Revolutionary songs, a few of the old political campaign songs, and the most popular songs of the War for the Union."

" And all of the songs that Tom Moore wrote while in America," said Charlie Leland.

" We would have a programme as long as a hotel bill," said Noble. " No ; we must select the most novel and pleasing."

Noble's instincts as to what is novel and pleasing, to the public at least, if not to the critics, were equal to those of a successful editor. The quaint old songs that he brought forth from the past surprised and delighted the Club. The Musical Society practised them daily, and the concert was appointed for the evening of February 22, Washington's Birthday.

As the Musical Society had only common gifts and culture, Charlie Noble's experiment was regarded by many members of the school as very unpromising; and it was evident that Master Lewis himself was wanting in confidence in it. The sharp remarks made by some of the boys in regard to the young candidates for musical honors compelled Charlie to use as much tact as possible in the selection of pieces and the manner of rendering them.

The first concert was given to the members of the school and their invited friends. The Musical Club numbered ten ; Noble acted as leader and conductor, and Charlie Leland as pianist.

There was a smile on many of the faces of the audience when the ten boys came upon the platform. The opening stanza of the song " Oh, my America ! " made the friends of the Club very nervous. Master Lewis looked straight at the toe of his boot.

But the refrain at the end of the second stanza arrested every one's attention. It was rendered with feeling. Then it was repeated softly and sweetly, with a real patriotic tenderness of voice and manner.

The audience was very still. Master Lewis raised his eyes from his boot's toe, — an object which had seemed to have for him an absorbing interest, — and applauded the effort.

Interest was awakened. The tender words " Oh, my America ! " had hardly ended when the ten boys astonished the audience by taking an attitude of enthusiasm and admiration, each holding out his right hand obliquely as though surveying mountain scenery. Then in a clear, resolute tone, they sang, —

> " The hills of New England, how proudly they rise,
> With their tall azure outlines, to blend with the skies !
> Romance dims their arches and breathes in the breeze :
> New England, my country, I love thee for these ! "

The last line was delivered in an oratorical tone, with an upward gesture of the left hand, and ended with a fine patriotic tableau in the attitude of the ten boys.

The pantomime was bold, graceful, and statuesque. All was interest now; even Master Lewis forgot his boot. At the end of the second stanza, beginning

> " The vales of New England, that cradle her streams,"

the hall rung with applause, and Noble found himself master of the situation. He smiled and bowed in response to repeated applause, and was inwardly so much delighted that a tell-tale expression stole over his face which said, " I told you so; " and the boys of the school, recognizing its import, burst into applause again.

" Adams and Liberty " followed. Then Otto sang, to Covert's music, Tom Moore's " Lake of the Dismal Swamp."

The ballad was told like a story, so artlessly that the audience was perfectly silent. Otto was recalled, and sang Locke's beautiful ballad

> " There 's a dear little mound by the willow,
> Where I wander at evening and weep ;
> There's a loved vacant spot on my pillow,
> Where a dear little face used to sleep."

At the words, —

> " Do I dream when in sleep I behold her
> With a beauty all new and divine,
> When so close to my arms I enfold her,
> And feel her warm lips upon mine,"

the audience was silent again.

Otto was again recalled, and sang a ballad of the same character, "The Old House at Home."

Noble was now sure of the interest and sympathy of the audience; and he began a little speech-making, giving a short account of the writers of the words and music of each song, and some of the occasions on which the song had been sung, as he introduced the title.

Of "Hail, Columbia!" he gave quite a history, which so interested the audience that it would have delighted in the song even had it been rendered less effectively.

Among the pieces were the "Blue Juniata," "Over the Mountain Wave," "Departed Days," "The Vacant Chair," "Do they miss me at home?" "The Year of Jubilo," "Alone by the Schuylkill," "Our flag is there," "A life on the ocean wave," "Be kind to thy father," "The Old Oaken Bucket," "Maryland, my Maryland," "Old Dog Tray," and "Your Mission."

"I did not know that we had so many songs of the heart in America," whispered Master Lewis to Mr. Beal, his assistant. "This concert is a credit to the school. I would not be ashamed to have it repeated anywhere. It has in it positive influence. It would make any one's heart tenderer. I must congratulate the boys."

He did so, most warmly. Noble had been gaining confidence all the evening, and now he was almost as tall as a full-grown man.

After Master Lewis sat down, the boys began to call, "Noble!" "Noble!" Charlie arose, bowed, and said, —

"The success of the concert this evening, if it be a success, reminds me of a story I once read of a young lady who did not receive much encouragement from her friends in her early days, but who nevertheless resolved to make the most of herself. I will relate it, and you may make such an application as you like.

"'Fanny Forrester' for some years was one of the most noted women in the country. When young she was a factory girl, and worked at splicing rolls.

THE JUNIATA.

" She, however, was allowed to spend a part of her time at school, and applied herself in her leisure moments out of school very closely to study. Her true name was Emily Chubbuck.

" When she was in her fifteenth year, her mother proposed that she should learn the trade of a milliner. Emily had nearly supported herself while at school by twisting thread and by sewing; but her love of learning was so strong, that while she was willing to earn her living from day to day during the time she was getting her education, she could not think of giving her life to anything but teaching.

" So she very decidedly protested against learning a trade.

"' But what do you intend to do?' asked her mother. 'You are almost fifteen, and cannot go to school always.'

" The family was poor, and Mrs. Chubbuck felt that it was necessary to take another step in the matter. So, a few days afterwards, an arrangement was made with the village milliner to take Emily as an apprentice.

" Dreadful intelligence was this, and Emily cried the whole of the night after she received it. The next morning she went to her academy teacher with a question that rested like a mountain on her mind.

"' Mr. B——,' she said tremblingly, 'do you think me capable of teaching school?'

"' Yes,' said he, smiling; 'you are capable, but you are not big enough.'

"' Will you please to give me a recommendation?'

"' Certainly.'

"' 'Not big enough!' Well,' thought Emily, 'that is not my fault, and I will stand just as tall as I can, and make the most of myself in this respect when I go before a trustee.'

" She was not fifteen years of age at this time, and very small in stature at that. Sickness had left its marks upon her, and her ability for managing a school must certainly have seemed doubtful.

"She told her mother that she wished to visit some friends living a few miles distant. As soon as she reached them she was told, in answer to her eager inquiries, that a teacher was wanted in an adjoining district. She started for that district at once, making a short cut across lots, and came to the house of one of the trustees. She rapped, and, dreadfully frightened, awaited a response.

"A raw-boned, red-headed man at last appeared in a red shirt, ragged pantaloons, and enormous cow-hide boots.

"The poor little applicant declares that she 'stood as tall as possible.'

"'Is a teacher engaged for your school?' she asked.

"The trustee looked at her with such evident astonishment that she at once lost heart.

"'How old are you?' he asked.

"'Almost fifteen.'

"The man puckered his mouth, and gave a great whistle. 'Whew! I will see the other trustees, and 'll let you know in a week or two,' he said at last.

"Emily knew what that meant. She turned from the house, made her way to some woods near by, and as soon as she was hidden from sight, sat down and cried.

"The next morning, however, one of her friends offered to aid her in her endeavors to obtain the school. They called on another trustee, — a very genial man. Emily presented her recommendation, which, in her fright, she had forgotten to show on the previous day. The gentleman thought favorably of her application, and advised her to see Mr. B——, who, he said, was the leading trustee.

"So Mr. B—— was at once called upon. He was a young farmer, full of good nature. He had a great troop of children about him, as most sunshiny people have.

"Emily made known her errand.

"'Why,' said he, 'the scholars will be bigger than their teacher.

Here, An't.' he continued, speaking to one of the children, 'stand up by the schoolmarm, and let's see which is the tallest. An't is the blackest, at any rate.'

"Emily says that she ' stood as tall ' as she could on these important occasions. Well, although she was so short, she obtained the school and succeeded.

"We are all trying to 'stand as tall as possible;' in other words, we are trying to make the most of ourselves. Good-night."

The audience saw the point of the story, and the impression was pleasing.

As Master Lewis passed Noble in the hall after the concert, he said, —

" I am willing that you should give a public performance after the Society has received a little drilling from the Music Professor; and I should be glad to have you make the experiment of a concert of American songs in the Provinces, should we make the tour you have proposed."

The Club gave three concerts in towns near Boston during the spring. Each concert was popular and successful. As the result, the Club had in its treasury $350 towards the proposed vacation trip. As the school year drew near its close, the principal topics of discussion among the boys were the proposed journeys in Acadia and New France

CHAPTER VI.

THE Class left Commercial Wharf, Boston, at eight o'clock one July morning, on the St. John steamer. The fare to St. John was reasonable for so long and picturesque an excursion, — $5.50. Late in the afternoon of the same day the boat touched at Portland, and then ran along the coast of Maine, traversing Passamaquoddy Bay. The sea was calm, the salt air cool, and

FISHERMAN'S HOUSE.

the scenes on the Maine coast a continuous picture. A lovely night followed a quiet day, and the coast of the province of New Brunswick came to view with the morning light.

New Brunswick is a quiet province; but she has a noble record for usefulness in the commercial accounts of the world. A pacific province that deals in what the world most needs is a benefactor of

THE LIGHTHOUSE ON GRAND MANAN.

mankind. There have been built in New Brunswick, during the past century, some ten thousand merchant-vessels, representing, possibly, $100,000,000. Her lumber trade and her fisheries are most useful occupations, and such as tend to make strong, worthy men.

The inhabitants of the province, some 325,000 in number, deserve high rank among the best communities of the times, on account of their pacific influence, useful industries, and moral and religious character. While loyal to the British Crown, their intimacy with the people of New England is very close and cordial. The tradespeople of St. John and those of Boston make their interests common, and there are goodly streets in Boston that are nearly half peopled by the former inhabitants of New Brunswick and Nova Scotia.

The province was a part of the romantic domain of Acadia. De Monts planted a colony here sixteen years before the coming of the " Mayflower " to Plymouth.

The principal points of its history are: The province was granted to the Sieur de Monts, 1603; it was first settled on the St. Croix, 1604. La Tour erected a fort at St. John, 1634. It was occupied by Cromwell's expedition, 1654; restored to France by Charles II., 1670; invaded by New England, 1703; ceded to England, 1713; conquered by Anglo-Americans, 1755–58; surrendered to England, 1765, by the Treaty of Versailles; disturbed by invasion, during the American Revolution. It became the abode of many American loyalists after the Revolution; was organized as a province in 1784; and one hundred years of peace and prosperity ensued.

At noon on the day after leaving Boston, the Class approached the rocky guard of the harbor of St. John. The hills came to view, — Carleton Heights and the Martello Tower.

St. John has been called the " Liverpool of Canada." Among commercial cities it holds the fourth position in the vast British Empire, — London, Liverpool, Glasgow, St. John.

St. John is so called from the discovery of the site on St. John's Day (June 24, 1604). It was the Menagwes of Indian tradition. Here Glooscap, the Indian god, whose Parnassus was Blomidon in Nova Scotia, had a residence. We are told that once, when he lived here by the sea, a wicked magician stole some of his people, and carried them to the islands along the coast. Glooscap pursued him,

INDIAN BEACH, GRAND MANAN

riding on the backs of whales. While on this expedition, he grew so tall that his head touched the sky. Of course he captured the poor magician, and released his friends. It would have been hard indeed to have escaped a pursuer who could summon the whales and grow tall like *that*.

CRUISING FOR PORPOISES.

The Class consisted of twelve boys, under the supervision of Master Lewis. Ten of these were members of the Musical Society; and of these ten, five hoped to pay in part the expenses of the journey by concerts of American songs in the cities of the Provinces.

On arriving at St. John, the Musical Club gave a free concert in the hall of the building of the Young Men's Christian Association, and the next day some of the boys sang at the Orphan Asylum. These free concerts awakened a popular interest in American songs. A concert was arranged to take place in the hall of the Mechanic Institute; five hundred tickets were sold, at a shilling each, with a clear profit of about $100.

The concert was a surprising success. So friendly are the people of St. John to the United States, that the audience encored nearly every national song, notwithstanding the disagreeable historic suggestions of some of the chords to provincial ears.

Master Lewis was touched by this simple exhibition of international good feeling, and, securing a British flag, asked Noble to close the concert with "God save the Queen," holding the flag from the staff in his hand.

Charlie Noble's tact was equal to any emergency, and he had provided for any such exhibition of good feeling as was found here.

Laying the flag upon the desk, he led the Club in singing "America." Then he surprised the audience by leading the old French rendering of loyalty, —

> "Grand Dieu! sauves le Roi!
> Grand Dieu! sauves le Roi
> Sauves le Roi!
> Que toujours glorieux,
> Louis Victorieux,
> Voye ses enemis
> Toujours soumis!"

He then took up the English flag, and, waving it, led the English national anthem, with a change in the words of the first two lines, —

> "Long live Victoria!
> Long live Victoria!
> Long live the Queen!
> Make her victorious,
> Happy and glorious,
> Long to reign over us.
> God save the Queen!"

Then turning to the audience he said, waving the English flag, — "All." The audience struck up, —

> "God save our gracious Queen,
> God save our noble Queen,
> God save the Queen!"

A part of the Class at the same time sung, —

> "Grand Dieu! sauves le Roi."

while Noble, in a clear soprano, like an obligato, sung, —

> "My country, 'tis of thee."

At the close of this novel chorus the audience burst into cheers, and the Class gave three hearty cheers for "the mother country and St. John."

LOW TIDE, ST. JOHN HARBOR.

A STRANGE STORY OF OLD ST. JOHN.

The history of Madame de la Tour is perhaps the most heroic and romantic of that of any woman who came to America during the French provincial period. One wonders, on reviewing it, at the strange changes that come into people's hearts and minds, and asks, Who can prophesy what may not happen in life?

Cadie— La Cadie — Acadie — Acadia! Before De Monts came to America, all of the colonies of the French Crown were called New France. De Monts's grant of territory embraced all the land lying east of the Penobscot, and so included the present provinces of New Brunswick, Nova Scotia, and a part of Maine. This grant was called Acadie; afterwards, Acadia by the English.

La Tour was a French Protestant. In 1625 King Charles was betrothed to the Princess Henrietta Maria, daughter of the French King. In the marriage treaty he ceded to France the whole of New Scotland, or Nova Scotia, which had been given to Sir William Alexander. Sir William sold the territory to M. de la Tour, who established a colony at St. John.

M. d'Aulnay, a French Catholic, acted as governor for the French Government in the territory between the St. Croix and the Penobscot. He was really a deputy-governor. La Tour and D'Aulnay were thus neighbors; and they became bitter rivals, with remarkable results, as the reader shall be told.

La Tour sought the friendship and trade of the people of New England, especially of Boston. D'Aulnay maintained the most intimate relations with the Catholic political party in France. In the religious wars of France La Tour of course sympathized with the Huguenots, and D'Aulnay with the Catholics.

Madame de la Tour was an intense Protestant. She threw her whole soul into the Protestant cause, and sought to win territory for Protestantism, as though she was commissioned for this work by Heaven. She was really a great woman in mind, heart, and conscience, and much her husband's superior, as we shall see.

La Tour built a fort at St. John, and D'Aulnay a fort on the Penobscot. La Tour began a very prosperous trade with Boston, which excited the jealousy of D'Aulnay. The latter was well versed in the French political art of intrigue, and he procured an order from the French Court for the arrest of La Tour as an outlaw and a traitor.

D'Aulnay organized an expedition against St. John. It consisted of several vessels and some five hundred soldiers. He blockaded the harbor of St. John, and besieged the fort, relying upon famine for its reduction.

La Tour and his wife escaped on a French ship, and came to Boston. Here they organized an expedition against D'Aulnay at St. John. It consisted of four vessels armed with thirty-eight guns, and a land force of resolute men. Madame de la Tour was the inspiration of the scheme and the expedition. She won the hearts of the people of Boston, and represented the expedition as a kind of Protestant crusade. She was virtually the generalissimo of the little armada. The fleet sailed out of Boston to take D'Aulnay by surprise. The latter was glorying in his success and triumphs, feeling a great sense of security, when the white sails of Madame's fleet, like awful apparitions, began to rise from the sea. He was compelled to flee to the Penobscot. La Tour followed him there. The squadron returned to Boston, and La Tour and Madame went to St. John.

Madame de la Tour next went to England to secure influence and aid for her husband's cause. She took passage on an English vessel for her return, the captain of which promised to leave her at St. John. The vessel made a circuitous course, and after a long voyage left her at Boston. She brought a suit against the master of the ship, and recovered the sum of two thousand pounds, — a very great sum for those days.

In the mean time D'Aulnay had fitted out vessels to prey upon Boston and other English commerce. It would not therefore be safe for Madame de la Tour to sail unprotected from Boston to rejoin her husband at St. John.

What should she do? She had means now, and she chartered an armed squadron to convey her to St. John ; and thus she again went out of Boston harbor like a princess, the commander of armed vessels and crews.

When D'Aulnay heard of this bold movement he felt the most intense anger. He had laid plans to capture the brave lady. He was humiliated at being outgeneralled by a woman.

" I will punish her yet," he said hotly.

D'Aulnay's wife was a proud woman, and was as ambitious as her husband for the capture of Madame and the destruction of St. John.

Madame de la Tour reached St. John triumphantly. There were no telegraphs in those days, and she found that her husband had gone away from the fort on a trading expedition.

Madame took command of the fort, and of the colony as well. Some Jesuits had established themselves there during her absence ; and she required them to change their abode, thus making the mistake of showing the same spirit of intolerance as her adversaries.

The priests of La Tour's colony were in sympathy with D'Aulnay. They informed him of the weak condition of the fort at St. John, and he resolved to make an expedition against it, and expected to capture it easily.

Madame was in command of the fort. D'Aulnay opened fire upon it, and to his astonishment the garrison, under Madame's orders, resolutely replied.

D'Aulnay renewed the attack vigorously. Madame's guns answered back so boldly that twenty of his men were killed, his vessel was riddled and dis abled, and he was obliged to retreat behind a bluff, repair his ship, and hurry back to Penobscot, defeated by a woman.

D'Aulnay was furious. His position was ridiculous. He saw that he would soon be a jest and a byword in Boston, England, and France.

"I will capture that artful woman yet," he declared. "She is the real cause of all our troubles."

The valiant ruler of the Penobscot at last learned that La Tour had again gone away on an expedition, and had again left the fort in charge of Madame. He mustered all the men he could command, fitted out another expedition, and hurried to St. John.

Madame de la Tour repelled the assault in the fort most bravely; but the garrison was small and was at last overpowered by superior numbers. The fort was taken, and Madame de la Tour became D'Aulnay's prisoner.

He took her to his fortified house at Penobscot.

As he conducted her into the hall, he said in a haughty tone, with the gestures of a courtier, —

"Madame, it gives me great pleasure to welcome you to my abode."

Then, turning to Madame d'Aulnay, he said in the same ironical but mock-courteous manner, —

"Madame, permit me to introduce to you Madame de la Tour. Her husband, as you know, is my greatest enemy, — except herself."

Madame d'Aulnay received the introduction coldly and proudly.

"I congratulate you," she said to her husband.

How strange is the sequel! Madame de la Tour died of disappointment and grief in a few days. De la Tour became a pirate. D'Aulnay died, and the courtly pirate, De la Tour, married the proud widow of D'Aulnay! This is not fiction.

After they were married, the romantic couple came to St. John, which Madame de la Tour had so bravely defended.

"*Your* husband and *my* wife used to have disagreements," said La Tour to his wife; "but those days are gone; let *us* live in peace!"

Here was a pirate chief whose soul is worthy of the monument of a dime novel.

St. John is situated near the entrance of the Bay of Fundy.

The Bay of Fundy, being narrow and open to the great Atlantic tidal wave, has the most wonderful tides in the world. At East-

D'AULNAY INTRODUCING MADAME DE LA TOUR TO HIS WIFE.

port, on the lower point of the bay, it rises twenty-five feet; farther up, at St. John, thirty feet; still farther, at Windsor, it comes suddenly rolling in to a height of sixty feet; and at Chignecto Bay the grand spectacle is seen of the sea rising over seventy feet in a short period of time.

The incoming tide at the Bay of Fundy is often dangerous to those engaging in shell-fisheries. At certain points the men and boys are obliged to run at the turn of the tide to escape from being drowned.

The swine on the upper bay, who feed largely on shell-fish, seem to know exactly when the tide is coming. They will venture out, in their quest for food, to low-water mark; but almost at the moment of tide-turning they will toss up their heads with a grunt of warning and run for the headlands.

The greedy pigs who linger a little over some delicious bivalves are not unfrequently swallowed up. The older swine take away the fat shell-fishes in their mouths, and may be seen climbing the headlands with them with a velocity that quite out-distances the tide.

Some years ago, an Irish family, fond of good pork and potatoes, moved to a point on the upper bay, taking with them some promising pigs, who had not learned the physical geography of the Bay of Fundy.

Pat's pigs for a time thrived delightfully on the shell-fish which he procured for them; but one day during the spring tides he concluded to let them run on the shore, which was lying, sunny and level, and spouting with bivalves, a very long distance below the high-water mark.

Pat knew little of the periodical ocean-surprises. In the course of two hours he saw his neighbors' pigs running violently, and was so amused at the sight that he stopped in his work to swing his hat and cheer them on.

He was pleased to notice that his own were not disturbed by the panic, and continued industriously at work.

Presently the sea was up to his knees; and he turned, like old King Canute, to remonstrate with the elements, which were as deaf to him as to the Danish King.

There was a foaming, a roaring, and a rushing; and Pat fled, being nearly overwhelmed by the tide before he reached safe rising ground.

"And sure," said Pat to his wife, "it's myself that left the craters fading at low-water mark, and thin the water broke loose and I run for me life; and when I reached the rocks the craters were rolling in the sea like porpoises, and the half of them is drowned."

FRANCIS I.

Physical geographists have attributed the tides of Fundy to certain inequalities in the bottom of the ocean. The high tide of the Atlantic Ocean at St. Helena does not exceed four or five feet, but, setting in obliquely on the coast of North America, it seems to run in a channel, or bed, gradually narrowing until it is stopped in the Bay of Fundy, approaching the head of the bay in an immense wave, whose coming is seen for miles. A roaring or rushing sound accompanies the advent of the tide, which heard from a distance is very sublime and overawing.

The shore formation of the bay for some hundred and thirty miles is an extensive sea-wall, which rises in stupendous precipices, and basaltic and green stone columns, three hundred or four hundred feet in height, thus opposing a barrier to the tides.

The tidal wave, in its greatest force and velocity, has rolled in the rocks from the sea, and piled them along the coast, as though building a barrier against its own destructiveness. The minerals found imbedded in the great water-trap thus formed are of great interest to the mineralogist, consisting of amethyst, rock-agate, chalcedony, rock-crystal, calcareous spar, and specular iron ore.

The high tides at Boston rise eleven feet; at Havre, France, twenty-two feet; at Liverpool, England, twenty-six feet; at Halifax, Nova Scotia, fifty feet; and at Chignecto Bay, New Brunswick, seventy-one feet.

The name *New France* was probably first given to Canada by Verrazano. The grand discovery by Columbus of the Western World led the maritime powers of Europe to send skilful explorers to the newly found coasts. The Italian mariners of the Mediterranean were intrusted with these commissions by all the European courts. Spain employed Columbus of Genoa; England, the Cabots of Venice; and Francis I., Verrazano of Florence.

Verrazano visited the Atlantic coast, from the Carolinas to Newfoundland, in the spring of 1524, nearly one hundred years

before the landing of the Pilgrims at Plymouth. He took formal
possession of the country in the name of Francis I., and called
the territory New France. The island of Rhode Island, then
blossoming in spring-time, greatly delighted him; and it is said
that he called it the Isle of Rhodes, in memory of the Isle of
Rhodes (or Roses), in the Mediterranean. He compares this island
with the Isle of Rhodes, in his journal. Hence the name *Rhode
Island.*

Verrazano was the first who saw the mysterious waters of
the North, unless they were previously discovered by the North-
men. This navigator lost his life in seeking farther to explore
the waters of the Western World.

CHAPTER VII.

THE Class left for Annapolis by sea on the steamer "Empress." In the warm weather this is a very pleasant route between the three principal cities of the Maritime Provinces, — St. John, Annapolis, and Halifax. Notwithstanding the great rise in the tides of Fundy, the water is generally so quiet that no sea-sickness is experienced in passing to Annapolis. The passage is made in some four or five hours; and the fare is, in English currency, about eight shillings, or two dollars. It is some sixty-one miles from St. John to Annapolis, and about one hundred and ninety miles from St John to Halifax. The full fare from St. John to Halifax is £1. first class, or about five dollars. A person may leave St. John at eight o'clock in the morning, and be in Halifax at the same hour in the evening. But any person with historic and poetic tastes will wish to remain a day or two at Annapolis.

Annapolis, the old Port Royal of Champlain, is a garden. It is situated on the Annapolis Basin. On each side of the Basin are mountains, and everywhere are fruitful orchards and well-tilled fields. It has only about twelve hundred inhabitants, and yet it is one of the most lovely summer resorts of the Maritime Provinces.

What a romantic history has this little town! There is nothing like it in New England. The Basin was first entered in 1604 by De Monts. The scenery enchanted the poetic and susceptible Baron de Pourtrincourt, and he secured a grant of the picturesque domain, and called it Port Royal. It was settled in 1606; and the leading mind of the new settlement was Lescarbot, the French poet, whose works still survive. The colonists built a fortress

VILLAGE STREET IN ANNAPOLIS.

here. They won the affection of a tribe of some four hundred Indians, whose chief was supposed to be a hundred years old. They taught these Indians Christianity, and induced them to live in a village near the fort. They built a palace here, and instituted the Order of Good Cheer. In the winter some member of this order gave a daily feast; and the Indians were invited, and the aged chief of a hundred years sometimes sat at the head of the table.

PROVINCIAL AND PICTURESQUE.

De Monts's grant was soon annulled by France, and the colony removed, leaving its fortress and palace.

There followed a series of most romantic events. The town, founded by a knight and by a poet, added chapter to chapter in a long poetic history.

BAPTISM OF INDIANS AT PORT ROYAL.

In 1610 Baron de Pourtrincourt sailed out from Dieppe with a colony again to establish a settlement in beautiful Acadie.

On arriving at Annapolis he found the palace and fort as he had left them. The Indians hailed the return of the French with joy.

The old chief and his tribe were converted, and were received

into the church amid the firing of cannon and the chanting of
Te Deums.

In 1613 Port Royal was destroyed by the Jesuits, who were
opposed to Pourtrincourt's liberal views.   Pourtrincourt was killed
in France a year or two after this event, at the battle of Méry-sur-
Seine.

CHAMPLAIN'S HOUSE AT PORT ROYAL.

In 1631 the domain was granted to Seigneur de Razilly, another
nobleman of dramatic history, and a relative of Cardinal Richelieu.
His lieutenants were D'Aulnay and Charles de la Tour, two adventurous noblemen, a part of whose singular history we have
already related.

In 1690 Port Royal was captured by Sir William Phipps, a

QUEEN ANNE.

man whose history more closely resembles that of Sindbad the Sailor than any other man's ever born in New England. We have already given a part of his history.

In 1710, after many changes, it came into possession of the English, and was named Annapolis Royal, from Queen Anne.

The Annapolis valley is filled with orchards. It is glorious with beauty and fragrance in May, when these are in bloom. It is claimed that fifty thousand barrels of apples are exported yearly from this valley, and that this fruit is the best in America.

The Order of Good Cheer, to which belonged Champlain, Pourtrincourt, De Monts, Lescarbot, and ten other courtly Frenchmen, enlivened each of their daily banquets with stories. The Indians on these occasions also sometimes related their traditions. Some of the Frenchmen gained a knowledge of the best Indian stories through interpreters, and repeated them to the Order. The Class gathered numerous stories of the period, and entered them in their note-books.

TALES OF THE ORDER OF GOOD CHEER.

"Let us imagine the old French times, before New England was settled," said Master Lewis to the boys, as they rested for an hour amid the ruins of the fortress,—ruins covering some thirty acres. "The fortress, whose history is ended, had not then arisen. There was only a rude French palace here.

"It is winter. Noon. A roasted deer is laid upon the table, and around it gather the old French explorers and Indian warriors. The meal over, Lescarbot recites a poem, and a French knight relates a story or some narrative he has learned from the Indians. We will suppose one of these to be as follows, an interpretation from the old chief:—

THE GIANTS OF THE ST. LAWRENCE.

In those far, dim periods that stretch so far into the past as to be almost beyond the imagination of men, there were two great worlds. One was a world of light, and was above; the other, a world of darkness, and was below.

Gods and goddesses lived in the world of light above, and hideous monsters in the world of darkness below.

Around the world of darkness were clouds and vast waters. The waters were also full of monsters.

Once in those far periods a wonderful thing happened, which caused the creation of the earth.

A light began to glow above the darkness of the lower world, and as it drew nearer, the monsters beheld the form of a goddess slowly descending towards them.

All the animals at that period had a language, and they began to consult with each other as to the manner in which the goddess should be received.

The turtles at that time were of enormous size, as large as islands are now, and one of these offered to receive the goddess on his back. The others were pleased, and covered the turtle's back with earth from the sea ; and it became a lovely field, full of trees and plants and flowers.

The goddess descended slowly, growing more luminous and beautiful, and at last after many years, as we now reckon time, came to the blooming island on the back of the turtle, and made it her abode.

Here she gave birth to two children, — twins. They were quite unlike in their character. One was benevolent, just, and perfect ; the other delighted in evil.

The first was called *Enigario*, and the other *Enigonhahetgea*.

The goddess died at their birth, and her soul ascended. Enigario, or the Good Mind, began the work of the creation of light, plants, birds, and fishes ; and his brother engaged in the creation of those things that are harmful to man. The Good Mind, finding that his brother was ruining the work of creation, overcame him, and drove him to the abode of dark spirits ; and he still lives there, and exercises his power over the evil souls that go from the earth.

Among the early creations was a race of giants. This race inhabited the North. After a time giants began to make pilgrimages towards the more temperate regions, and a band of them discovered the Great River (St. Lawrence).

SETTLERS AND INDIANS FEASTING AT QUEBEC.

A gentler race, called the Eagwehoewe people, had been created ; and they dwelt on the Great River and its beautiful seas. They greatly feared the giants of the North, and hid from them when the latter came down to the summer regions from the lands of the frozen oceans. The giants robbed them, destroyed their homes, and carried them away captives.

Among these gentle people who lived on the Great River in the land of summers was a family of princes, consisting of six brothers and a sister. The father of this family had been renowned in war, and had died on the field of battle.

One day the six brothers went into the forest to hunt, and left their sister alone in her airy palace in the shadows of the mountains on the Great River. They had scarcely gone, when the sister saw the head of a man towering among the trees. Birds were flying about him, hawks and crows. She knew that he was one of the giants of the frozen lands of the North.

The giant discovered the palace. The sister tried to escape ; but he caught her, and, seeing that she possessed wonderful beauty, he treated her very kindly, and told her that one day he would make her his wife, and that they would live together in his own gigantic palace in the crystal regions.

The lovely princess greatly admired the giant ; and she fell in love with him, and readily consented to go away with him from the Great River and the land of summers to his palace in regions of the crystal seas.

When the six princes returned home from their hunt, they were filled with sorrow to find their sister gone ; and they knew that one of the giants had carried her away.

"I will follow the giant," said the eldest of the six.

Far, far to the north sped the prince ; and he came at last, just as the sun was setting, to the giant's palace.

He there discovered his sister ; but when she saw him, she hid, and the prince knew that she had fallen in love with the giant.

He entered the giant's palace. The giant received him kindly, and offered him a pipe, and the two talked together in a friendly way for some hours.

Now the giant was a wonderful musician.

"Go to bed," said the giant at last, "and I will play you a tune on the pipe, and sing you to sleep."

The prince retired, and the giant began to play and sing. The room was warm, as the giant kept a roaring fire ; and the prince, who had travelled far, soon fell asleep. Then the wicked giant killed him in his bed, and hid his body in a cave.

The five princes, finding that something had detained their brother, consulted what they should do. The eldest of the five said, —

"I will go and find my sister and brother. Stay you here."

But a long time passed and he did not return.

Then said the four princes, "What shall we do?"

"I will go to the North, and find my sister and *two* brothers and bring them back. Stay you here."

But he did not return.

Then said the three, "What shall we do?"

"I will go to the North, and find my sister and *three* brothers, and will bring them back. Stay you here." So said the eldest of the three.

But he did not come back.

Then the two princes said, "What shall we do?"

"Stay you here," said the elder of the two. "I will go and find my sister and *four* brothers, and bring them back!"

But he did not come back.

Then the youngest set out in search of his sister and *five* brothers, and came to the giant's palace in the land of the crystal seas.

This prince, although the youngest of the family, was brave, wise, and strong. The giant received him graciously.

"Where is my sister?" demanded the prince.

"She is my wife."

"Where is my eldest brother?"

"I have sent him to visit my people."

"Where is my next eldest brother?"

"I have sent him to join the other."

"And my next?"

"I have sent him to join the *two.*"

"And the next?"

"To join the *three.*"

"And the next?"

"To join the *four.*"

"When will they all return?"

"After you have rested."

Then the giant prepared a bed for the prince, and warmed the room, and said, —

"You shall hear me sing and play, but first retire. To-morrow you and your brothers will be together."

THE PRINCESS AND THE GIANT.

Now the prince was wise. He feared that his brothers were dead, and that he would, if he slept, indeed be with them on the morrow, where their bodies were concealed.

So he said to the giant,—

" Let me go into the woods to gather an herb, for I am sick, then I will go to rest."

The prince went into the forest, and secured two bits of firewood about

the size of the pupils of his eyes. He returned to the palace, and lay down in the bed, and the giant began to play and to sing.

When the prince felt sleep stealing over him, he put the two bits of fire wood on his eyelids; and the giant, after he had ceased to sing, looked at him, and thought that he could see the light of his eyes, and that he must be awake.

The giant watched him all night, but thought he could see the light of his eyes.

The prince arose the next morning and walked into the great pine forest. He followed the path of the giant, and came to a great cave. There he found the dead bodies of his five brothers.

He returned to the palace, attacked the giant, and slew him. The soul of the giant ascended, and was changed into a star. The sister fled into the forest, and died of grief. Her soul ascended, and was changed into the Star of the North.

This story ought to be true, as you can see the star now.

" Let us suppose the pious Champlain to be the next story-teller. His thoughts go over the seas for some incident that will turn their thoughts to the life within and the life above.

THE PALACE OF PRAISE.

The lights were going out in the old palace at Achen. There had been a banquet. The courtly knights were gone, — the palgraves and palgravines.

The young King of Aquitaine sat at the deserted tables. The room was empty ; even the minstrels and court fools were gone.

The feast had celebrated a conquest, and the conquest had crimsoned the Rhine. It celebrated a war of ambition, crimes, and desolation. The young king, Aquitania, was a guest ; he had been gently educated by Father Joseph, and the outpouring of wine to celebrate the outpouring of blood had been a shadowy spectacle to him.

In the dim light of the fading astrals a tall man in a dark robe came into the room. It was Father Joseph, the young king's adviser, who had come with him from Aquitaine.

The two went into the chapel. It was late at night. The clock had already struck the hour whose strokes recall the apostles.

The priest read the lesson. It was from a Pauline epistle : —

" Some men's sins are made manifest before the judgment, and some men's sins follow them to the judgment. So, also, the good works " —

Aquitania listened.

— " of some men are made known ; but the good works that are not now known cannot be hidden, — time will reveal them."

The priest had amplified the text, to make the meaning clear to the boy king. He added: —

"The soul is building. Some men are building for themselves prisons in the coming life; some, palaces of praise. Evil deeds turn into prisons, walls, and chains; good deeds into palaces of praise. The influence of good deeds goes on forever, and the palace grows. Whatever you may lose, my son, do not forfeit *that* palace. They that be wise should shine as the sun."

A short prayer was said. The next day the two went back to Aquitaine.

Years went on. Aquitania ascended the Carlovingian throne. He became a famous king, — famous for his misfortunes, for the losses of crowns and kingdoms. His losses came through his unselfishness. His people loved him, and it was said of him, "He loves others better than himself!"

He sent missionaries to the North. They changed barbarous tribes to Christian kingdoms.

Ambitious men conspired against him, and he lost his throne. Discrowned though he was, his almsgiving went on. His influence was an empire in itself, — an invisible kingdom. It made men love God.

He went to a lonely rock on the Rhine to live alone in peace, to pray and to die.

Father Joseph came to him there.

"My son, you have lost your crowns and kingdoms."

"My father, do you remember your lesson in the old palace chapel at Achen? I have not lost my Palace of Praise."

Years passed. The lights shone in the castles on the hills at night; his island was torchless. The summers filled the grapes with wine; the wine filled for him no golden goblets. War boats went by; he did not hail them, or ask whither they were going.

One night he lay dying under the stars.

Peacefully.

Father Joseph was there.

The vision of the old banquet rose before him when he was a fair-faced boy and King of Aquitaine.

"Father Joseph, am I dying?"

"Yes, my son."

"I am going to the Palace of Praise."

The Rhine flowed on, sobbing as it went out into the night, past the luminous castles, to the sea.

The sceptreless hands were folded now; the crownless head at rest. God had crowned his life with another life. The Rhine flowed on.

His Palace of Praise was not completed. Churches multiplied in the North; Christian kings came out of the old missions. Poor men spoke his name, and, as often, it made them better. The world for centuries has been carrying jewels to his Palace of Praise.

The lights have gone out in the castles on the Rhine: the old palace at Achen is gone; but the Palace of Praise, we may fancy, grows more beautiful in that kingdom which is not of this world.

"They that turn many to righteousness shall shine as the stars —

"Forever."

"The good deeds that are not now known cannot be hidden, — time will reveal them." The Rhine flows on.

"We will now suppose that Lescarbot recites a poem. I cannot give one of his poems here, nor an imitation of one. You may find some of them in the Boston Public Library: at least, the Ode to Champlain.

"Next the old Indian interpreter speaks: —

THE RETURNED SOUL.

It is night.

Look up. It is bright. The stars are in the sky. They grow brighter as you ascend. The sun is above us. Glorious is the pathway towards the sun.

Glorious is the pathway towards the sun. Moca made the journey, and found it glorious. The celestial regions are there: the land of fire. There night does not come. They are not weary there. Those who go there do not wish to return.

They do not wish to return. Do you wish to go back to childhood, and be rocked again by the winds in the trees? Do the old desire to go back to the labors of middle years? Who would call back the dead to this lower world?

Who? Moca did. He loved too strongly. He had but one child. That child was a son. He was noble and brave, — fair to look upon. His name was Ona. His plume led the braves. Wherever he went, his father's heart went with him.

His father's heart went with him. Ona died, — his soul went to the regions of the Summer Maker. Moca's heart went there too. Moca laid his dead son in the earth; the squaws wailed over him; the braves wrung their hands; the maidens covered the place with the shells that sing of the sea. But Moca's heart was dead to the earth; it followed his son's spirit, that had ascended to the high lands and the bright lands. Moca dreamed of the bright lands. He looked up to the star lands at night, and the sun lands by day. When the cloud lands only appeared, Moca looked down and wept. He said: "Oh that I could visit the sun lands! Would not Pap-Kootparout give me back again the soul of my son, my only son? The sun lands! the sun lands! They are happy in the sun lands. The wells of light are there!"

The wells of light. When Moca basked himself in the sun, he said: "I am drinking from the wells of light! My heart is there. Ona is there. They say that those who go there do not wish to come back. I am going to make a journey to the sun lands and ask Pap-Kootparout for the soul of Ona. Oh for one hour with the soul of Ona! It is a beautiful way. I am going. Oh for one hour amid the blessedness and brightness where Ona dwells!"

Blessedness and brightness! The old warrior called to him two trusty friends. "I am going to the star lands and sun lands," he said, "to ask for the soul of Ona. Will you go with me?" They were ready to go. They prepared themselves by fasting and prayer. They started one morning. The morning was fair.

Fair. A blue lake of air lies between the earth and the sun land, — a great sea. The waters are light in the sea of air. They are not deep. Moca and his two friends took with them poles to make a platform on which to sleep. In the day they journeyed under the sun lands, and at night they slept under the star lands. The sea of air grew brighter and brighter as the three went on.

Brighter and brighter. They ascended above the mountains, then above the regions of the birds. At night they spread out their poles, and made platforms above the waters. Every day grew more splendid, and every night more glorious; and at last they looked down, and the earth was far, far away.

Far, far away, — an island in the sea of air. And above, in the same sea, the stars changed to islands of gold, and the sun to a palace of fire. The sun lands appeared. All was brightness and fragrance, song and bloom. The three travellers were happy. Said Moca, —

"I have never seemed to live before. My soul expands, — it is glorious!"

Glorious. But as they crept up to the shaded groves on the shore of the sea of air, Pap-Kootparout beheld them, and came running towards them. His face was terrible. He lifted a war club above his head, and swung it in the air.

"Back, back!" he shouted. "Go back and leave your bodies in the earth. You cannot come with such perishable garments here. Back!"

"Back?" said Moca. "Do you know a father's feelings?"

"A father's feelings? Are you a father?"

"A father? I was once a father, but my son is here, — my only son. I have come to ask from you the gift of his soul. You will not refuse me the gift of the soul of my only son. Let me take it back or remain here."

"Remain here? That cannot be with those miserable garments. Come and see the land. Have with me a game of ball."

The three travellers had a game of ball with the god. The god lost his terrible expression, and his face grew shining and glorious. The three travellers won the game, and the god invited them to his shining palace to partake of a celestial feast.

The celestial feast was over.

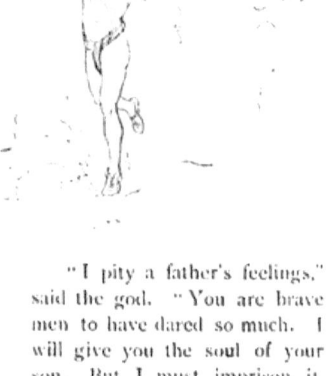

"I pity a father's feelings," said the god. "You are brave men to have dared so much. I will give you the soul of your son. But I must imprison it. He would never be happy on the earth again. He would fly upward if he were to escape. I must give you the soul in a bag, or earthy garment like your own. Do not open the bag. But when you return to the earth again, put the bag and the soul in the body of your son. He will then stride forth a great and glorious warrior, and be the champion of your race."

A champion. Moca's heart rejoiced. He received from the god the bag, and hurried back to earth over the thin sea of air. His soul became sad and heavy as he came near the earth; and his companion said, "Would that we had never gone on the journey, for we can never be happy again!"

Never again. They came to the earth. They gathered together the nation, and told the story of their ascension to the palaces of bliss. Then Moca gave the bag and the soul to a squaw to keep, while he went to disinter the body of his son. Never such a wonder happened in all the land.

Never. Moca came back with the body. The sun shone bright. The braves shouted, and the maidens danced for joy.

But the joy did not last. The squaw to whom had been intrusted the keeping of the bag had a great curi-

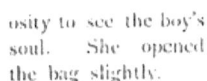

osity to see the boy's soul. She opened the bag slightly.

There was a voice within.

"Let me see the sun." She opened it wider.

There was a voice in the air, — "The sun! the sun! He cannot dwell on the earth who has been to the sun. You will follow me soon. The sun! the sun!"

The soul had flown away, — ascended. Moca followed it soon to the land of the sun, leaving his perishable garments in the earth.

"Such, we may fancy from the old voyagers' journals, was one of their feasts, or at least a semblance of it.

"I know of nothing more curious and romantic than the banquets of this old Order of Good Cheer in the palace of Port Royal."

CHAPTER VIII.

ACADIA.

HE Halifax train to Windsor passes through orchards and quiet villages. The traveller is charmed by the poetic names of places as well as by the pleasing views. Romance is in the air. He hears of Gold River and Gaspereaux Lake. One of the towns is called Paradise.

The tourist on his way to Halifax will, of course, stop over for a day or two at Wolfville or Grand Pré, and visit the Land of Evangeline. The visit may best be made from Wolfville, a town with possibly a thousand inhabitants, having three hotels with lovely names, — "Village Hotel," "Acadia," and "The American," — all of which owe much to their nearness to Grand Pré, made immortal by Longfellow's pen. Acadia College (a Baptist institution) is here, and Acadia Seminary, and Horton Academy. The town has the atmosphere of refinement and intelligence, and is among the few Acadian places that have a forbidding name.

The college buildings are situated on a hill overlooking the Basin of Minas. From the belfry of the college one may see one of the most beautiful views in the Maritime Provinces, and certainly the most famous poetic locality in the country, — Grand Pré, or the Great Meadow reclaimed from the sea; the majestic bluff of

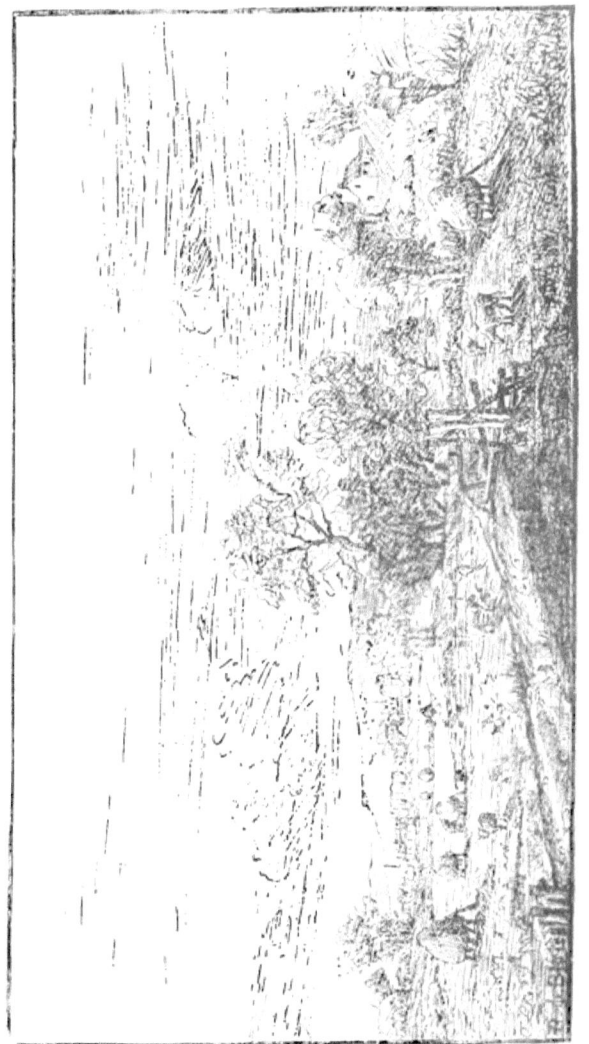

GRAND PRÉ.

Cape Blomidon, and the Basin of Minas shining like burnished silver in the sun.

THE STORY OF ACADIE.

Grand Pré, — the Great Prairie or Great Meadow, — a most lovely and fertile valley, is situated, as every lover of Longfellow's pastoral poem knows, on the Basin of Minas. Quaint dikes used to restrain the sea on its border : for here are felt the sudden forces of the wonderful tides of the Bay of Fundy. Over the idyllic meadows rises Blomidon. It was one of the most lovely settlements of New France, with its hundreds of thatched roofed houses and white chapels. Its inhabitants were peaceful, light-hearted, and pure minded people, and, like the patriarchs of old, lived by pastoral occupations. Having no ambitions beyond the cultivation of their fields and the care of their families, religion was their life, — a religion free from the selfishness and barbarism of their English neighbors of the time.

After the conquest of Acadia by Sir William Phipps, the land had a brief rest under the English flag. Then came the Chevalier Villabon from France, and hauled down the Red Cross and ran up the White Lilies ; and Acadia found herself again under the protection of the parental crown. Having retaken Port Royal for France, Villabon proceeded to recover all the old French territory from the Bay of Fundy to the Penobscot.

The re-conquest led to another invasion by the New England colonists, led this time by Colonel Benjamin Church, famous as an Indian fighter and as the slayer of King Philip. This man's piety has been much exalted, though on what grounds it would be hard to tell, as his conscience never seems to have told him that selfishness and cruelty were wrong, that even savages have feelings, and that peaceful Catholics were entitled to his love and respect. He seems to have championed the cause of an imaginary Deity, and to have quite overlooked the Sermon on the Mount and Christ's teachings in regard to the Samaritans. It was he who mutilated King Philip's dead body, and caused it to be made a dreadful spectacle in the domain where that defender of the rights of his race nobly perished.

A single incident will show how wrong views of life had turned this man's heart wellnigh to dust.

One night he invaded a small island on Passamaquoddy Bay. The inhabitants, French and Indians, made no resistance.

"Looking over a little run," says Colonel Church, "I saw something black. I stopped and heard a talking. I stepped over and saw a little hut or wigwam, with a crowd of people around it, which was contrary to my former directions.

"I asked them what they were doing. They replied that there were some of the enemy in a house who would not come out.

"I hastily bid them pull it down *and knock them on the head*, never asking whether they were French or Indians, *they being all enemies alike to me.*"

Yet this man, who had so little sense of justice or mercy on an occasion like this, was heroically conscientious about matters of slight importance.

The Acadians were not only a peaceful people, but were honest and truthful ever in their dealings with the Indians. Their history is darkened by no broken treaties and by no forest tragedies. The Indians were always their friends. To them the red man was a brother. The priest labored to convert him, to make him wiser and better, and never sought to defraud or destroy him. The principle that Champlain had set forth, that the conversion of a single soul was of more value than the conquest of an empire, prevailed. The Acadian magistrates could never, like certain magistrates of New England, have offered "fifty pounds for each woman *and child scalped*" in a time of trouble with the native races. The Acadian had a different heart. The Acadians and Indians were brothers. The Indians were to the Acadians what Massasoit was to Roger Williams, when the latter was driven into exile, and sought the hospitality of his lodge at Mount Hope.

Church saw the beautiful valley of Grand Pré, its peaceful homes and holy chapels. Here was an opportunity for him to do his duty, as he interpreted it.

MASSACRE OF THE INDIANS BY ORDER OF CHURCH.

The fact that the people were non-resistants was nothing to him. He burst upon the settlement like a beast upon its prey; and the simple cottages of the Acadians vanished into smoke, and blackness and desolation wrapped the land.

After a time the Acadians returned to the valley. The dikes were built again. The sea meadows again were green.

The province of New Scotland, or Acadia, passed under various treaties. Now the English Cross floated over it; now the Lilies of France. Grand Pré grew until it became a town of eighteen thousand souls.

The account of the Acadians given in Longfellow's "Evangeline" is hardly overdrawn, if we may trust what the Abbé Reynal wrote of them. Nearly all of them owned houses, thatched by their own hands. They pastured some sixty thousand head of cattle. They raised their own wool, and manufactured their own clothes. Almost every family owned horses, cows, and sheep.

They had little or no money, and needed none. Poverty was unknown. If one were unfortunate, he had a common home with the whole community. Instead of being an outcast, he was adopted by all. There were no crimes. The priests settled the few difficulties that arose. The churches were supported by all the people, who contributed for the purpose one twenty-seventh of their harvests.

Grand Pré, without any false poetic colorings, came near realizing an almost earthly paradise. It certainly was one of the purest and most unselfish communities that has had even a temporary existence. Any man who could have desired the destruction of such a community must have had an eye as pitiless as a rock, and a heart as hard as selfishness can render it. But the invaders came.

It was September, 1755. The harvests had been gathered, and the barns were bursting. The community had never before been so happy and prosperous.

As *neutrals* in the contest between England and France, they had taken the oath of allegiance to their English conquerors, but had refused to take the oath to bear arms against their own countrymen. The Indians also would not promise to bear arms against the French.

One bright day, just as summer was changing to fall, there appeared in the glorious harbor of Minas five or more ships. They were under the general command of Colonel John Winslow, who, we are sorry to say, was born in Massachusetts, and brought from that colony a body of armed men to carry out the despotic order of the king.

Winslow landed, and issued a proclamation to the people to assemble in their church at a certain hour of the day, saying he would then make known to them a new order from the Crown.

EVANGELINE.

A part of the proclamation read as follows : —

"We therefore order and strictly enjoin by these presents all of the inhabitants, both old men and young men, as well as all the lads of ten years of age, to attend at the church at Grand Pré on Friday, the fifth instant, that we may impart to them what we are ordered to communicate to them.

"JOHN WINSLOW."

The poor people, unused to deception, filled the church. Only men were admitted within the walls. Longfellow pictures the women as waiting outside in the churchyard on the lovely autumn day, and as garlanding the graves of their ancestors, while the king's order was being promulgated.

The communication that the deceitful lips of John Winslow had to make crushed the life out of the heart of every Acadian who heard it. A part of it was as follows : —

"It is peremptorily his Majesty's orders, that the whole French inhabitants of these districts be removed; and I am, through his Majesty's *goodness*, directed to allow you the liberty to carry off your money and household goods, etc."

They were prisoners in their own church. The scenes that followed cannot be described. The men, unconscious of any crime, begged permission to be allowed to visit their families once more. With a few ex-

DEATH OF KING PHILIP.

ceptions this was denied. There were not one Gabriel and one Evangeline; there were thousands.

The road from the chapel to the shore was a mile or more in length. Over this the men were marched to the ships. Says an historian :—

"The young men were first ordered to go on board one of the vessels. This they refused to do, declaring that they would not leave their parents. The troops were ordered to fix bayonets and advance upon the prisoners.

THE BASIN OF MINAS.

"The road from the chapel to the shore was crowded with women and children, who on their knees greeted them, as they passed, with their tears and their blessings, while the prisoners advanced weeping, praying, and singing hymns. The detachment was followed by the seniors, who passed through the same scene of sorrow and distress."

The whole male population of Grand Pré were thus put on board of the five transports ; and every woman's heart followed her husband, brother, or son, as Evangeline's feet are represented to have gone out after Gabriel. The village was left in flames. Truly

> " Nought but tradition remains of the beautiful valley of Grand Pré."

It has vanished from the earth. An aged willow is shown that is said to mark the site of the shop of Basil the blacksmith. The road taken by the exiles on their heavy-hearted way to the king's ships is pointed out. The place is colored with romance by its historic associations and the poem.

It is said that Longfellow would never visit Grand Pré, lest it should destroy his own ideal. He need not have cherished this fear. The scene of the tragedy is a place of superlative beauty. The sea, the mountain, the orchards, the prairie, all have a wondrous charm when the summer fills with splendor the Basin of Minas and the meadows of the sea.

Acadia is still to be found in Louisiana, with its traditional homes of simple religious faith and true affections. The Acadians have had little to disturb their quiet habits in the lands beneath the warm, sunny skies of the South.

CHAPTER IX.

ALIFAX is indeed a city of the sea. Its harbor would hold the navies of the world. No other natural harbor surpasses it; it is the pride of the Province, in which pride England shares. It is always accessible, always safe; and a thousand ships might pass and repass at the same time. Here are to be seen the flags of all nations on peaceful errands of trade.

Halifax is not a great city. It does not number quite forty thousand inhabitants. Its site is noble. The city stands upon a peninsula, and is literally founded upon a rock.

It rises to a height of two hundred and fifty-six feet from the water's edge, and is crowned by a citadel. In some of its features it resembles Quebec.

The citadel was begun by the Duke of Kent, the father of Queen Victoria. The water view from the citadel on a fair day is one of the most noble and delightful on the coast. The calm harbor, the distant fog-banks, the deep color-line, the islands, the far-off hills and primeval forests, the dock-yard with its display of England's naval power, the city with its thick spires, combine to present a view that long holds the eye and leaves its impress on the memory.

It is a rich city. Its merchants are not men who have acquired sudden wealth, but have gained it by useful enterprises and honorable dealing.

St. John is almost an American city. It is as social and democratic as a new town of the West. Americans like St. John, and St. John's people seem to like Americans.

Halifax is British and aristocratic. The presence of military forces tends to foster this feeling. No city could be more loyal to the Crown.

The Public Garden is most beautiful. The remains of the once splendid estate of the Duke of Kent recall very dramatic associations. The old Province House was once the finest building in North America.

In the summer of 1746 the French armada, consisting of some forty ships-of-war and thirty transports, and an army of thirty-one hundred soldiers, sailed out of Brest, under orders to occupy Louisburg, reduce Nova Scotia, and destroy Boston. The fleet was dispersed by unparalleled storms. The commander, the Duc d'Anville, reached Halifax with only two ships. The ruin of the expedition caused the duke's death; and the vice-admiral committed suicide for the same reason. It may be well in this connection to speak of

QUEEN VICTORIA AND THE ENGLISH COLONIES.

In June, 1884, Queen Victoria completed the forty-seventh year of her reign, which began on the 20th of June, 1837, the day on which King William IV. died. She completed the sixty-fifth year of her life twenty-seven days earlier, May 24, 1884.

Thus far the reign of Victoria has been fortunate, though she has had her share of the disappointments and afflictions that are incident to every human life. As compared with the reigns of most monarchs, hers may well be thought eminently successful, both personally and politically. A long reign is considered evidence of good fortune in a sovereign, though some very good sovereigns have very brief reigns.

Tried by this last consideration, Queen Victoria may be classed as a very fortunate monarch. There had been, previous to her ascension to it, thirty-four sovereigns on the English (later, *British*) throne since the date of the Norman Conquest (A.D. 1066); and of these, only six had long reigns.

VIEW OF HALIFAX HARBOR.

The exceptions are, Henry III. (1216-1272), Edward III. (1327-1377), Henry VI. (1422-1461), Henry VIII. (1509-1547), Elizabeth (1558-1603), and George III. (1760-1820).

The length of her reign exceeds those of all her predecessors but Henry III., Edward III., and George III.; and if it should be extended to the beginning of 1897, her possession of the throne would be longer than that of all her predecessors, as then she would have entered upon the last half of the sixtieth year of her reign and the seventy-eighth year of her life.

No English sovereign has reigned sixty years. The longest reign of any English monarch was that of George III. He was given, also, the longest life. He died in the sixtieth year of his reign. Henry III. ascended the throne when he was but nine or ten years old (1216), and died in 1272. Edward III. died in the fifty-first year of his reign. Henry VI. was dethroned in the thirty-ninth year of his reign. Henry VIII. reigned almost thirty-eight years, and Elizabeth more than forty-five.

Victoria has sat upon the throne longer than any sovereign of the Anglo-Norman line (1066-1154); longer than any of the Angevine line, commonly called Plantagenets (1154-1485), excepting Henry III. and Edward III.; longer than any sovereigns of the Tudor line (1485-1603); longer than any of the English sovereigns of the Stuart line (1603-1689); longer than the two sovereigns of the Nassau-Orange-Stuart line (1689-1702); longer than Anne (1702-1714); and longer than any sovereign of the Hanoverian line (1714-1873), excepting George III., who was her grandfather.

It is proper to form an opinion of the possibility that hers will be an extended life and a long reign, from the character of her family in respect to longevity.

George I., first king of the Hanoverian line, died at the age of sixty-seven, in 1727, and in the thirteenth year of his reign. His mother, Sophia, Electress of Hanover, lived to be eighty-four.

George II. died at seventy-seven, in 1760, in the thirty-fourth year of his reign. His eldest son, Frederick, Prince of Wales, who never became king, died at forty-four, in 1751. He was great-grandfather of Queen Victoria; and his wife did not live to a great age.

George III. died in his eighty-second year, George IV. in his sixty-eighth year, and William IV. in his seventy-second year.

The Duke of Kent, father of Queen Victoria, died in his fifty-third year. Her mother, the Duchess of Kent, died at the age of seventy-five. Some of the queen's relatives, descended from George II. and George III., lived to be old.

The average length of the reign of Victoria's thirty-four predecessors (counting William III. and Mary II. as one, for they reigned jointly) is under twenty-three years, and she has already exceeded that average by more than one half, and she may treble it.

Some sovereigns of Continental Europe have had very long reigns. Louis XIV., of France, died in the seventy-third year of his reign, and Louis XV. in the fifty-ninth year of his reign. Ferdinand I., of the Two Sicilies, reigned almost sixty-six years. Frederick III., Emperor of Germany, reigned about fifty-three years. Probably all these long-reigning monarchs found out the truth contained in the words of the old Spanish poet: "Those who know most of life know most of care."

HER COLONIES.

The great orator and statesman of the last century, Edmund Burke, once boasted that England rules over an empire "on which the sun never sets." He meant that throughout the twenty-four hours the sun in his course was shining upon some part of the British dominions, and that in every part of the globe were to be found countries and colonies which acknowledged allegiance to the British Crown.

This is even more true to-day than it was when Burke made the famous vaunt. Since his time England has gone on sending out and establishing colonies here and there, until now that "right little, tight little island" holds sway over no less than one third of the surface of our earth, and Queen Victoria's subjects comprise nearly a fourth of its entire population.

England, indeed, has been the greatest and most successful mother of colonies among modern nations. She has rivalled Rome in the creation of colonial communities, and has spread her power, as Rome did, by planting little nations of her own people wherever she could get a foothold.

Other modern nations have attempted to create colonies, but this has usually been without success. Holland, Spain, and Portugal have to some extent succeeded; for the Dutch still have flourishing colonies in Java and Sumatra; the Spanish colonized Mexico, Central America, and many parts of South America; and the Portuguese once had powerful colonies in the East.

France, Germany, and Italy, on the other hand, have never been successful in making colonies; and the United States have never as yet tried the experiment.

The possessions of England over the globe comprise an area of four and a half million square miles, thirty times the area of the island of Great Britain itself. The territory contained in British America is much larger than that included in the United States. England rules over a million square miles in Asia, and two and a half million in Australasia.

GEORGE I.

BURKE.

On every continent her flag floats over some colony or province; and in all she has no less than thirty-nine colonial provinces and groups. In Europe she holds Gibraltar and the islands of Malta and Heligoland; in Africa, the island of Ascension, the colony of the Cape of Good Hope, the gold coast of Guinea, Mauritius, Natal, and other places; in Asia, the islands of Hong Kong, Ceylon, Labuan, and Parim, besides the mighty Empire of India, and a number of settlements in China and the Archipelago; in Australasia, Australia, New Zealand, New South Wales, and Feejee; in America, all the territory north of the United States except Alaska; the Bermudas and Bahamas, Falkland Islands, Jamaica, Guiana, Honduras, and many islands.

For over two hundred and seventy years this system of colonizing has been carried on by the English. As long ago as in 1605 she took possession of the

Windward Islands ; and she is even now adding to her list of colonies on the African coast.

The English colonies are divided into three classes, according to the way in which they are governed. The "Crown colonies," among which are Jamaica, most of the African settlements, and India, are governed entirely by the home government at London, which makes and executes their laws.

The "representative colonies," among which are the Bermudas, Natal, and Western Australia, have their own parliaments, while the home power appoints all the officials Finally, the colonies with "responsible governments," which include Canada, the Cape of Good Hope, and the Australian colonies, not only make their own laws, but appoint their own officers, the Crown being represented by a governor or governor-general.

Napoleon once said to Fox, pointing to a terrestrial globe, "See what a little place you occupy in the world!" He would not make a like remark were he living to-day. No colonies are more loyal to the queen than is the vast Empire of Canada, and no city in America is more thoroughly imbued with patriotic devotion to the Crown than Halifax.

There has been a great deal of discussion in England during the past few years, whether it is not best to give such colonies as desire it their independence. Nearly all the English colonies, indeed, now have free institutions, and are practically independent ; they yield little pecuniary profit to the home power, while that power has the burden of defending them from attack.

The general conclusion seems to have been reached that when the colonies themselves desire to dissolve the bond between them and the mother-country, and become nations, the latter will not object ; but the colonies are slow to give up the advantage of British protection from assault, and as yet none of them have shown a very earnest disposition to be independent.

A CONCERT THAT THINNED THE HOUSE.

The success of the concert in St. John gave the Class great confidence of like results in other cities. Charlie Noble did not consider the fact that as St. John is a city of strong American tendencies and sympathies, and as the concert had been advertised by the free concerts, the result was the simple relation of cause and effect.

"SEE WHAT A LITTLE PLACE YOU OCCUPY IN THE WORLD!"

"We shall have a house in Halifax that will open Master Lewis's eyes," said Charlie, on the day of the boys' arrival at the old provincial capital.

He was right. It did. It opened the eyes of the Class as well, and Charlie's own eyes, but hardly in the way that he had expected.

The night of the concert was favorable. The Class arrived at the ante-room at eight o'clock, and soon after entered in procession by a side door.

The hall looked like a chasm.

Charlie stopped in amazement in the middle of the platform, and said to an usher.—

" Where are all the people gone."

" *Gone?* They — they — they are not here *yet.*"

There were just twenty persons in the hall, and of these nineteen were in the gallery. The floor was occupied by one solitary man, — a fat, jolly-looking old gentleman. He pounded his cane on the floor as the boys came upon the platform. The hall echoed the gracious old gentleman's applause, as though it had been a hollow cave.

Master Lewis came upon the platform. His eyes were opened, as Charlie had predicted.

He said to the boys in an undertone,—

" Give as good a concert as though the house was full. Imagine an audience, and do your best."

" Oh, my America " was well sung. The hollowness of the galleries and the emptiness of the floor gave the loud tones a very oratorical effect. When the *pianissimo* part was reached, and the words " Oh, my America," were finding a lodgement among the arches, a broad voice whispered in the gallery,—

" The boys are crying for home; hear them, — ' Oh, my America ! ' "

Charlie Noble grew red in the face.

After the first piece the old gentleman who occupied all of the lower floor, again thumped with his cane, and there was a dead silence.

The Class sang " New England," and the good-natured old gentleman thumped again.

" The Red, White, and Blue" seemed greatly to please the solitary old gentleman, and it was applauded by the scattered people in the gallery as well.

" Now give us ' Yankee Doodle,'" said a voice in the gallery.

Just at this point there was an appalling interruption; five of the nineteen persons in the gallery got up and left, leaving fourteen.

Charlie Noble's face wore an expression of bewilderment.

" ' Yankee Doodle ! ' " called several voices from the gallery.

" ' The tune that the old cow died of,' " called another voice.

Charlie's face blazed.

" When the British evacuated Boston," said Charlie, " it was to the tune of ' Yankee Doodle.' As you ask for it *again*, we will now sing it."

The song was given, but with some misgivings. The old gentleman thumped tremendously.

An evacuation followed, that illustrated the old adage that " misfortunes never come singly." *Seven* more people arose and left, and there now remained but nine people in the hall, including the old gentleman.

After " The Lake of the Dismal Swamp" had been sung, two more people rose, and left vacancy behind them, so that now there remained but seven.

" Do they miss me at home ? " was very feelingly sung. Two more of the audience vanished into the land of mystery, and now there were five.

" The Vacant Chair " seemed suggestive of vacancy, and two others left; three now remained, including the generous old gentleman, who continued to thump after every song.

VICTORIA.

"When shall we three meet again?" had the doleful effect of causing two more to follow those who had joined the great outside world, and the old gentleman was left all alone.

"Let's sing 'The Fine Old English Gentleman,' and then go to the hotel," whispered Charlie.

This song seemed greatly to delight the audience of one. The audience applauded loudly.

The boys made their farewell bow; and before they had filed out of the side door, the sexton had turned off the lights.

"I hate Halifax," said Charlie.

"Hush!" said Master Lewis, "we are ourselves to blame. Had we used the same methods as in St. John, the result would have been the same, or at least better than now. Results follow effort in concerts as in all other things. The lesson will be worth something. I am glad that the old gentleman enjoyed it."

The next morning, a note was received at the hotel for the "American Boys." It read briefly,—

Boys,—Stand by your flag. I always have by mine. You did well yesterday. I learn you are on the way to Quebec. I enclose passes. Better luck next time.

THE OLD ADMIRAL.

The passes were on the Steamship Company. They were worth at least a hundred dollars.

"So the concert was a success, after all," said Charlie. "It was worth the concert, to meet such a good soul as 'the Old Admiral.' I think I would like Halifax."

LOUISBURG.

For the erection of the fortress of Louisburg, France paid thirty million livres. A hundred years ago it was the great fortress of America. To-day it is a sheep pasture. Would that every fortress could be transformed with safety into a field at once so useful and so

picturesque and poetic! The sheep pasture of Louisburg in summer
is a most delightful place.

A broken sea-wall of hewn stone, the outlines of a vast amphitheatre,
a glacis, avenues amid buried ruins, still remain. The green grass
grows over all; and there the sheep peacefully graze, and shepherd-
boys watch them, while the cool winds temper the heat of the sun. A
noble harbor lies under the eye; afar is the limitless sea.

The fortress did not leap into life. It was built to hold an army,
and it cost the labor of twenty-five years. The walls rose to a height
of thirty-six feet, and were nearly three miles in circumference. Its
foundations were laid immediately after the death of Louis XIV., and
it was named in honor of Louis XV.

We can see it in fancy as it loomed over the Bay, with its embra-
sures for a hundred and forty-eight cannon. It was both a fortress
and a military town. On an island in the harbor was a battery of
thirty cannon, and at a point of the harbor was another battery of
twenty-eight guns, most of them forty-two pounders. There was a
church in the fortress, and over all floated the Lilies of France.

A light-house gleamed from the high cliff; sentries paced along
the walls; the harbor was filled with the war-ships of Louis. And
here New France was deemed impregnable; here she held the key of
the Great Gulf, and here she hoped to protect forever the richest fish-
eries of the sea. Little did the solemn sentry of a century or more
ago dream of the ruin of to-day.

It took two years to blow up the immense walls. The result of
this two years' labor still appears in an outline of the walls. Green
mounds of earth cover all. Louisburg is like a graveyard. It is the
tomb, rather than the ruin, of a fortress.

The Class made an excursion to the ruins of the once proud fortress, and then returned to Halifax. The excursion led Master Lewis
to relate some interesting historic stories in relation to Louisburg and
the settlement of Halifax, one of which is given here.

LOUIS XIV. IN OLD AGE.

THE OLD HOUSE ON CAMBRIDGE COMMON.

It was in July, 1843, and the evening before Washington Allston's funeral. I arrived in Boston late in the afternoon, and immediately started for Old Cambridge, where I expected to spend several days, attend the memorial service of the poet-artist, and witness his interment in the historic churchyard.

The old house in Cambridge where I was to pass the night stood near the colleges, on the very ground where the Shepard Memorial Church now stands.

My friend Kenyon, whom I was to visit, had told me something about the place. It had belonged to a family by the name of Moore. Deacon Moore was a prominent man in colonial days and during the Revolutionary period, and was the treasurer of Dr. Holmes's church, as I shall soon have occasion more particularly to explain.

I had heard Kenyon say that from the windows of the house a crowd of bright eyes had witnessed the cavalcade that conducted Washington to Cambridge. The old elm stands only a little distance from the place under which the young General, in 1775, took command of the army.

Lombard poplars shaded the house in front, if I remember rightly, — tall, spectral trees, on which the moonlight was falling. There were two porticos, between which the visitor was expected to make a choice according to his social rank or station ; at least, it had been so in a former day, and the house suggested still a colonial rather than a republican code of etiquette. But I was not obliged to make choice between them, as my friend was expecting me, and stood waiting for me in the deep, cool shadows before the open door.

After supper we entered the roomy parlor, where the windows were open and the lights turned low, and talked of our school-days and old friends who were changed and gone.

My feelings were somewhat mellowed by the subject. There was a stillness about the room, the house, and the colleges, which impressed me ; and I suddenly recollected that I had heard Kenyon say, when we were school chums, that there was some strange mystery associated with the place. I reminded him of the remark, which began to awaken a deep curiosity in my mind, and asked, —

"Was the mysterious person supposed to be old Deacon Moore?"

He smiled faintly, and said : "You are tired and nervous, and we will pass all that now ; these old stories have not been revived for years. Nearly every old house in Cambridge that outdates the present century has its legend ; and this,

14

DEACON MOORE'S HOUSE.

I believe, is no exception to the rule of traditional ghost-lore, but in that respect is rather a remarkable estate. But strange old Deacon Moore has ceased to walk nights, if indeed he ever was troublesome ; and the mending of outhouses, doors, and fences is now left wholly to carpenters. How the story of the deacon's ghostly wanderings used to unnerve me when I was a boy ! I pity one," he continued, " who is subject to nervous fears. There is one room in this house that I used to dread, though I cannot tell why. My impressions, I have always noticed, have some association with reality. This impression — the dread, the fear, I used to experience on spending an hour in that room — seems to be causeless, and yet I have a feeling that more cause for it may yet be discovered. But it will hardly do to dwell upon this subject, for we are to spend the night in that very room. There is little danger that the old nervous horror will return upon me again, especially in your company. I used to suffer the most from it, if I remember rightly, when my mind was not fully occupied, and when I had been excited with much company and suddenly left alone.

The place was once my study and sleeping-room, but I have not slept there now for many years. It has been fitted up for me again, while a part of the house is undergoing repairs."

Kenyon rose to go into another room, asking to be excused that he might speak with Mr. Gennison before the family retired.

He was gone a long time; and when he returned, he proposed that we should go at once to our room, saying he knew I must be tired.

The room was large, quaint, and old-fashioned; and there was something in the remarks that Kenyon had made that immediately interested me in it.

It was a still, lovely night; and the moon, now risen in full splendor, covered the colleges and churches like a sea of haze, and barred with long lines of light the uncarpeted floor. I do not know but the moonlight heightened the effect of Kenyon's suggestions of some mysteriousness about the apartment, — romance so frequently associates moonlight with what is mysterious; but, however this may be, my feelings impelled me to ask further questions, although the subject had evidently become distasteful to my friend now that we were in the room.

"Did you once think the room was haunted?" I ventured.

"No, not exactly that," he said curtly; "still it used to seem to me that there were shapes and objects in it that could be felt rather than seen, — something wrong, something that ought not to be. There will be many artists and literary men in town to-morrow. We hardly appreciated Allston here; he led such a quiet, dignified, retired life."

"Are there many old houses in Cambridge famous for legends or ghost lore?" I resumed.

"Yes; there was the Vassall house (Longfellow's), and the Royal house at Medford, and — "

"But this house, you said it held a first rank in old colonial superstitions, I believe?"

"Not in colony times, but after that."

"Was it reported to be haunted?"

"Would you sleep more quietly if you knew?"

"Yes; truth is better than suspense."

"After Deacon Moore died some peculations were found to have been committed."

"Well?"

"Well, the deacon was a very restless man before he died. He had a strange habit of wandering about the premises nights, with a hammer or hatchet in his hand, repairing outhouses and fences, and making the neighbors very unquiet at unseasonable hours."

" Well ? "

" Well, after he died, it was discovered that he had been in the habit of appropriating money to his own use from the church treasury, and suspicion fell upon his character.

" Well ? "

" Well, *the sounds continued.*"

" What sounds ? "

" Oh, the hammering and the thumping and the driving of nails in the night."

" But you surely do not believe that any such disturbances were caused by the disembodied spirit of Deacon Moore ? "

" No, I do not ; I am not superstitious enough for that. The deacon was a very singular man, I am told, especially in his last days ; and when suspicion fell upon his character after his decease, he was just such a person as superstitious minds would at that period expect to return in ghost form to haunt the place. And as his mending of buildings and fences nights was one of his most annoying characteristics, it is not strange that natural sounds occurring late at night should be attributed to his hammer. The event caused great excitement in its day, and nervous people for a long period avoided the place in the night.

" But," he continued, " although I do not believe any such silly stories as the old people used to tell, I do believe in my own impressions ; and I have had a fixed impression for years that there is something wrong about the place, and when I am in my most sensitive moods the mystery seems somehow to be associated with this very room. You may think me over-sensitive and credulous ; but I suffered from vague nervous impressions when I used to occupy the place. I have had an indistinct dread of it since I left it, and I would not sleep in it again to-night if you were not with me. I would not like to sleep in a room where I knew some great crime had been committed ; not that I would expect to be troubled by the victims, but because I am sensitive to the associations of a place. I would rest better in a room where a good man was married than in one in which a bad man died. With many it would make no difference ; but I cannot help this peculiar element implanted in my nature."

The old Cambridge clock struck the hour of twelve. We ceased talking. The wind arose, to sing the newly leaved branches of the trees, and causing dark shadows to move with an uncertain motion across the floor. With an unquiet feeling I watched the shadows for a time, and then began to feel the sweet influences of sleep.

The next night Washington Allston was buried in the old Cambridge churchyard. Brown, the landscape painter, must remember the scene ; he was a pupil of Allston, and, if I remember rightly, was among the torch-bearers when the remains were uncovered, and the moon breaking through the clouds shone full upon the face of the dead.

After the funeral I returned to the house, and inquired for Kenyon. I found a note from him, saying that he had been detained in Boston, and would probably be compelled to remain there during the night. I am not superstitious ; but the vision of my sleeping-room and Kenyon's dread impression of it immediately rose before me, and I am free to confess that I did not enjoy the prospect of passing the night alone.

I was lonesome without Kenyon, was tired, and I went to my room soon after returning, thinking I would lounge in a very inviting easy-chair, and read until I became too drowsy to be at all influenced by the solitariness of the place or my constitutional nervous fears. I say constitutional nervous fears ; for I, like Kenyon, was susceptible to more influences than I could see, hear, or define ; and I too had observed that impressions received when I was highly sensitive almost always found some counterpart in reality, or met with some rather remarkable fulfilment.

It was a partly cloudy night, with an atmosphere full of fragrance, and a glorious moon. The few now living who attended Washington Allston's funeral must distinctly remember it, — the parting clouds, the shadows anon shutting out the soft moonlight, the lights on the college grounds, the still, warm air.

I leaned out of my window, as the first relief from my solitary situation. Christ Church broke the view of the churchyard, where the poet-artist had just been laid.

A strange subject forced itself upon my mind, — a subject upon which, so far as I know, no books, essays, or poems have ever been written, — the fate of the loyal refugees of Boston and Cambridge during the Revolutionary War. Some of them went to Barbadoes, a few returned to England ; but many went to Halifax.

Halifax at that time was a military town, though it had not yet become an English fortress. Many of the movements of the English forces against the colonies were directed from Halifax. The old provincial parliament of Halifax, a body hostile to the American cause, met in 1770, and continued in session fourteen years. Halifax then promised to become a great military city.

The Boston and Cambridge royalists, when they incurred popular displeasure and found themselves in danger, fled to Halifax over the easy waterway. The phrase, " You go to Halifax !" as an expression of contempt and a suggestion of profanity, became common among rude people.

Did these royalists ever return? But few of them. The democratic feeling was so strong during the period that immediately followed the war, that all who had opposed the American cause were treated socially as traitors and enemies, and both their property and their lives were in danger. At the close of the war most of the loyalists who had remained in Boston during the conflict went

THE OLD CHURCH IN CAMBRIDGE.

to Halifax. The old city was largely founded by English colonial loyalists and refugees.

The grand harbor of Halifax made her a naval port, and a resort of the old defenders of the Red Cross on land and sea. But Halifax has derived her fame and wealth from the peaceful fishing-fields that lie spread out around and before her, rather than from those of martial achievement. The heroes of her ships have been men of peace.

But to return to my curious narrative.

I was wandering in dreams through the dim vistas of the past, catching, as it were, glimpses of forms long faded and gone, never to see the July sunshine or the green earth again, when a sudden sense of some mysterious influence began to steal over me. I can only describe it as a feeling that there was something that ought not to be in or about the room. I saw nothing, heard nothing; yet there seemed to be near me the presence of something impalpable, a dark presence, an atmospheric chill and gloom. "I am growing nervous," I thought; and I flung myself upon the bed.

Did I dream? I cannot say. I seemed to be dreaming, and yet conscious of my dreams, — to have a double consciousness, a double sense of things. The dark impalpable presence seemed to descend, and then began a dream or semi-consciousness of supposed circumstances that were extraordinary. It seemed as if a mason was building a vault under the floor. I fancied I could hear the rattle of bricks, the splash of mortar, and the click of a trowel.

I started up; the dream passed away. It was a bright night, and the wind breathed refreshingly through the trees. I was vexed at my own nervousness, and presently was half asleep again.

But in that debatable condition between sleeping and waking the same sounds seemed to be repeated, — the fall of bricks, the splash of mortar, the click of the trowel. I tried to think of Kenyon and old school-days. The click of the trowel became fainter; I heard the clock striking twelve, and fell asleep.

Towards morning I was roused by a passing wagon in the street. It could have been but a moment between sleeping and waking, but in that moment the same vivid dream was repeated. I fancied I could hear the sound of masonry under the floor.

Fully awake, I heard nothing, and my sleep had been sweet and undisturbed. Towards morning I found myself drowsy again, when the click of the trowel again startled me. I started up, threw myself into the arm-chair, and sat there undisturbed until the morning began to redden in the east.

Kenyon returned before noon, when I went with him to Boston, and took leave of him there.

I never forgot the impressions of that night, though I did not tell Kenyon of them. I seldom recall dreams, and I cannot relate any dream I ever had in my life, except that one so vividly repeated. As I have thought of that, I have had a horror of nervous disease, for it fixed in my mind the conviction that no suffering could be more dreadful than nervous apprehension and fear.

Many years passed before I saw Cambridge again. I have not the exact date now, but it was the year when the building of the Shepard Memorial

Church began. The old Charles River bridge had given place to a more substantial structure, as I noticed when I passed. Kenyon was in Nevada, and
the old Moore house was uninhabited, and was soon to be taken down. The
land on which it stood was to be used by the Society of the Shepard Memorial Church for their new building.

I was at my hotel one evening, when a newsboy entered the hall, and said, —
"*Journal! Traveller! Herald!* Startling discovery! Two bodies found
in a vault of the old Moore house!"

I started to my feet. I bought a copy of each of the papers, the *Herald*
giving the most detailed and curious account. The paper described the situation of the room ; and I felt a nervous perspiration steal over me, as I identi-
fied it as the very apartment that Kenyon had occupied, and about which he
had given me such an unfavorable impression, and in which we had passed
the night together, and I had dreamed the one vivid dream that stamped itself indelibly on my memory.

I immediately went to the place. The house was partly taken down ; and
a great crowd of people were around it, and within the admissible part of its
ruins.

I went to my old chamber, forcing my way with an air of special concern
through the crowd. The floor was taken up ; under it was an open brick
vault. It was empty. Men and boys were talking about the "bodies." I
received the most unsatisfactory answers to my questions about the discovery,
and turned to the policeman who had taken charge of the place.

"Where are the bodies?" I asked.

"The old skeletons? They have been removed."

"What is your opinion about them? Violence?"

"Well, the bones are so old you can't tell. They may be, for aught any
one knows, a hundred years old. This is a very old house, and they used to
tell some curious stories about it a very long time ago. People got the idea
it was haunted; people used to believe in such things more than they do
now."

"Did any two persons ever disappear mysteriously from Cambridge
years ago?"

"Not that I ever heard of."

"But how could such a vault as this have been built without exciting
suspicion?"

"I don't know."

He presently added, "Anatomies, perhaps."

"But why were the skeletons hidden in such a room as this under the floor? Why were they placed in a vault at all?"

"I don't know. It all looks kind of mysterious." And with an easy air, that showed that mysterious things were not unfamiliar to him, he walked slowly away.

The vault was nearly under the place where my bed had been on the nights I had occupied the room, and where probably Kenyon's bed had stood when the room was his study.

Old people associated the discovery with Deacon Moore. The stories about his strange habits, and his supposed peculations from Dr. Holmes's church treasury, and about the mysterious noises on the premises after his decease, were again revived, and old New England superstition for a few days seemed to start into new life in the town. A case of circumstantial evidence, throwing suspicion upon the eccentric deacon, was at once made up; but it seemed to have but little basis in fact, and the same suspicion would doubtless have fallen upon any other singular person who might have long ago occupied the house.

The leading incidents of this story are mainly true, and will readily be recognized; and I would not, for the sake of heightening the effect of a plot, do injustice to the memory of one who may have been a wholly innocent man. I can but remember, in associating tales and rumors with facts, that old New England superstition threw a shade of suspicion over many an innocent name.

It is a Cambridge mystery, and it gathers around it the gloom and romance of nearly one hundred years. Who are these people? Were they brought to their hidden tomb by the hand of violence? If so, why were they placed in a vault in a private house, where time would surely disclose the secret of their burial and raise the darkest suspicions? Were they anatomical specimens? Then why were they hidden at all?

The old Moore House is gone; the historic church of Dr. Holmes is gone; spire and one of the finest of the churches of Cambridge now raises its finger-like spire over the spot where the mansion of the mysterious deacon once stood. I sometimes pass the place in my evening walks; and the old tradition and more recent mysterious discovery return to my mind vividly; but it is all an association of the past,—of times dark and ended, faded and gone.

I have but one theory that promises a solution.

Halifax, as I have said, was settled largely by royalists from America during the War of Independence.

Among the latter were people who are known to have lived a short time in the new city, but who often expressed a strong desire to return to their friends in Boston. These people during their stay at Halifax helped the British cause in many ways, and incurred the bitter enmity of many of their old-time friends in Massachusetts. Some of them disappeared mysteriously from Halifax, and were never again heard of there. They had relatives or friends who lived at Cambridge. Were the bodies those of these refugees?

It ends in mystery. A mysterious story it will always remain. I was led to associate the story with the refugees only on account of my impressions that night, and that from the circumstance that a part of my impressions was afterwards proven true. The narrative at least will give you a glance at old Halifax and the possibilities of old colonial times.

CHAPTER X.

THE audience at the concert at Halifax somewhat shadowed the golden dreams of the Class. After the success at St. John, the boys had expected to find all the cities of Canada awaiting them with open purses.

"Shall we give a concert in Quebec?" asked Charlie Noble of Master Lewis, on the steamer.

"Quebec is French," said Master Lewis. "Montreal, Ottawa, and Toronto would be more likely to be pleased with American songs than Quebec. In all matters of this kind adaptation is the secret of success, — *tact*, as you yourself have said. Suppose you learn a few songs of emigration. They are American; in the places I have named they would be likely to touch the popular feelings. Such songs as Mackay's "Cheer, boys, cheer!" "Far, far upon the sea," "Land, land!" "To the West! to the West!" "The Pioneers," the "Canadian Sleigh Song," would be pleasing in the Provinces, I should think. We shall remain a fortnight at Quebec. You will have time to practise these songs there."

"We *must* succeed," said Charlie. "Like Fanny Forrester, we must make the most of our opportunity, and 'stand as tall as possible.'"

"What good would that do, even if you could touch the stars, if there were no one to see you?" said Robertson.

" There will be an audience to hear us next time," said Noble.
" You will see."

He was right again.

GASPÉ.

The scenery on the Gulf of St. Lawrence between Chaleur Bay
and the river St. Lawrence is bold and wonderful. Here is a coast
that tourists and writers have little visited; it will be one of the
romantic summer resorts of the future, when some vivid author or
painter shall unfold its beauties to the world. A Starr King would
see it with the eyes of a discoverer. Grand Manan has begun to
draw tourists to its castle-like coast; Mt. Desert has become a summer city. Gaspé and Gaspé Bay await the time of recognition of
lovers of sublimity and beauty; to the few travellers who visit them
now, their very obscurity has a charm.

" Boy," said an old steward to Charlie Leland, " I see you are a
lover of scenery. You may be now on the look-out for a sight that
will surprise you. You will wonder why you never heard of it
before."

The boys were all eager listeners to the steward's direction; they
were leaving Cape Despair, and expected soon to see Bonaventure Island. A rock began to attract their notice. It rose from the
sea like a dark pillar. As they drew nearer to it they were astonished at its immensity. Soon a more remarkable feature met their
view — a rock that formed a lofty arch. It was like a ruin of a
colossal church, whose tower in proportion might have reached to
the sky.

" Perce Rock," said the steward, — " five hundred feet long and
nearly three hundred high."

" No obelisk or ruined citadel could be more awe-inspiring than
that," said Master Lewis.

Behind the rock rose a dark mountain with a broad top like a plateau. The mountain, the rock, and the waters of the Gulf

A NATIVE.

formed a tableau so majestic and grand that the Class looked upon it with amazement; and the wonder grew as the ship was passing between the cliff and the island.

"What a spectacle it must be by moonlight!" said Master Lewis to the steward. "There are few combinations of scenery in the world that can equal this. Nothing is more noble on the Rhine."

"See the clouds of birds above the rock!" said Charlie Leland. "There are thousands of them. They seem to be having a battle in the air."

PERCÉ ROCK.

The red sunset was flaming beyond Mt. St. Anne. Bonaventure Island, some three miles long, — a vast pile of reddish cliffs from three to five hundred feet high, breaking a tide fifty fathoms deep, — was sinking into shadow. Through the mighty arch appeared the luminous levels of the sea. The air was still; the gulf, calm; the sky, clear. The cloud of birds settled down upon the rock, and the ship steamed on in silence as through a solitude.

The waves of unnumbered centuries have beaten Bonaventure Island. Its high walls are fretted by the storms of countless winters and the assaults of breakers, the tide-impelled waves at times rushing upon them like an army of horsemen. The sea will conquer in the end, and the rock will disappear, after the battle of ages!

A dark cloud arose in the crimsoned air from the high rock. Then uprose a gray cloud. The air was filled with a din of discordant cries.

"The gulls and crows are at it again," said the old steward. "They never keep peace for an hour at a time. If a gull trespasses

COMMON GULL.

on the colony of the crows, why, the parent birds of both kinds just fly up in the air and fight it out. Curious, ain't it?"

"Do they live there?" asked Charlie.

"Yes. The top of that rock is a great meadow; it is covered with grass. The whole of the upper part is full of nests, — cormorants and gulls. A few years ago," he added, "the boys found a way to climb up to the top by ladders of rope; and since that time egg-hunters have gone up every spring. The gulls' eggs are useful; but I always thought there was something mean about robbing these birds'-

nests. The gulls confide in the sailors so. You have seen them
follow ships, almost come on board; gentle-like, — tame. Well, you
would n't believe it; when the fishermen and boys go up to get their
eggs, the birds are that confiding that they do not rise from their

* CARTIER ASCENDING THE ST. LAWRENCE.

nests, and they utter a cry of disappointment when their eggs are
taken from under them. I would hate to rob one of their nests.
Gulls bring good luck."

"What a glorious sight!" exclaims Arthur Baies, in writing of
Gaspé Bay. "Imagine a bay, twenty miles long, ending in a basin
where a fleet of a thousand vessels might be sheltered!"

Gaspé may be the oldest town in America. It is believed that
Norse vikings had a fishing station here long before America was

discovered by Columbus. The Spanish mariner Velasco is supposed to have visited the bay in 1506. Cartier came here in 1534, and here formally took possession of the country in the name of his church and king, erecting a cross thirty feet high, adorned with the Fleur-de-lis.

THE "PHANTOM" OF ISLE PERCÉ.

As the boys were leaving the ruins of that once grand castle of nature, the rock island called Percé, the red light was fading in the west, and the shadowy glooms of the Canadian woods, so peculiar and suggestive at nightfall, began to appear among the hills. Suddenly a bright, shimmering light filled the air above the great stone arch, now in the distance.

"The phantom," said the stewardess, coming out of the cabin.

"The wings of the sea gulls rising into the light of the sky," said the steward. "'The phantom!' Woman, whom do you take us for? Do you think these American gentlemen have ears for old fishermen's stories?"

"They have eyes," replied the woman, sharply. "Look, yonder. *We* all know what that means. Never you mind what *he* says; it is the phantom of the rock. See there now; it is vanishing."

"The birds have settled down from the high air on to their nests again," said the steward.

"That's what *you* say it is," replied the woman, with cold light in her eye. "The old belief in the saints is going, and those who wish to think that they have no friends in the spirit world are welcome to their loneliness for all me."

"But, madam, what do *you* say it is?" asked Master Lewis.

"I don't say. But *we* all think it is the good spectre of the rock."

She continued: "Years ago, — more than a hundred, — there lived in France an officer who loved a beautiful girl."

"Now, woman!" said the steward.

"They were about to be married, when the officer received an unexpected order to sail for Quebec. He obeyed, but left his heart behind him."

"First man that I ever heard of who lived without a heart," said the steward, lighting his pipe.

"As soon as he reached Quebec, he sent for his bride."

"To bring him his heart, I suppose," said the steward, puffing his pipe.   .

"She sailed for Quebec on receiving the message. But the ship was captured by a Spanish pirate; and all the crew, except the young bride, were put to death. The girl was exceedingly beautiful."

"No doubt," said the steward. "Her beauty shone like the gulls' wings up in the air."

"The captain of the pirate vessel wished to make her his wife, and told her that she must consent or die.

"'Then I will die,' said she. 'My heart is pledged to another.'

"'Think of my demand a week,' said the pirate.

"'I will die if need be, but I will die true to him to whom I have given my promise.'

"'Then you shall see Quebec, but you shall never land there. You shall pass by it, and not meet there your lover; you shall return by the Castle of St. Louis, and then you shall perish.'

"The ship was approaching the river St. Lawrence, as we have been during the afternoon. In the twilight a form was seen floating on the sea. It disappeared. It was the captive bride.

"The ship approached the Rock Percé at nightfall. As the sailors were wondering at the formation of the cliffs, — there were two arches then, one of them is now gone, — what should appear against the

THE TRADITIONAL PHANTOM OF PERCÉ ROCK.

black stone-wall but the form of the bride, like an angel all clothed in white!"

"Woman!" said the steward.

"And what became of the ship?" asked Charlie Leland.

"She began to turn into stone from that moment. She grew heavier and heavier, and sank lower and lower in the sea. Her sides became a rock, and her masts iron-like, and her sails slate;

LACHINE RAPIDS, ST. LAWRENCE.

and she began to drift towards the rocks, and became a part of them.

"The captain and the sailors all turned into stone. The stone ship was to be seen, perfect and entire, for more than fifty years."

"Woman!"

"It's a fact. There are the ruins of her to be seen to-day, off Cape Rozier. We shall pass *her* in the night, or I would show her to you. Husband don't believe in nothin'. Good-night. Hope you'll all have pleasant dreams."

The morning found the Class in the river St. Lawrence, moving slowly towards Tadousac.

Sunrise on the St. Lawrence is a splendor never to be forgotten. It seems like a light flashing on a world of waters, for the very pines drip with fog and dew. There is a crystal brightness everywhere. The sun grows into full-orbed glory through a veil of mist. It seems like a morn of the early world.

The ships and canoes in the thin fog on the smooth tides, the grayish gulls that follow the steamer, the silence everywhere, the loss of all apparent motion of the steamer, give one an experience that is at once novel and unreal. One recalls here such legends as " Undine," and the pictures of Turner and Doré.

THE SAGUENAY.

The Class landed at Tadousac, one hundred and thirty-four miles from Quebec. Tadousac is a small village on a terrace. Below it is a fine harbor; around it are mountains. It has a noble hotel on a bluff.

"It seems like an eagle's nest," said Noble, in reference to the hotel. So seems the town.

The view from the escarped height is noble; the dark mountains, the sombre Saguenay, the immense St. Lawrence.

Tadousac was founded in 1599.

The class here took the Quebec steamer for Chicoutimi, the farthest port on the Saguenay.

The Saguenay is unlike any other river in the world. It is a mountain chasm, — a river of colossal shadows, silent, ancient, and lonely. The gray cliffs of gneiss seem like the monuments of giants.

The Saguenay reminds one of the fabulous rivers of Chaos; when the tourist comes back from it, he seems to have returned from the primeval world. It has been likened to the fiords of Norway, but its grandeur is distinct. There is but one Saguenay.

Chicoutimi is about one hundred miles from Tadousac.

You enter the river, and no living thing is seen. The waters are deep and black. You recall the fable of the Styx. The river is frozen half the year. It is a dead river, a Lethe.

THE MAL BAIE RIVER AND LAKE.

About half-way between Tadousac and Chicoutimi is Eternity Bay, walled by majestic cliffs. The water here is one hundred and fifty fathoms deep. Cape Trinity and Cape Eternity are masses of rock, which seem to rise from the black waters to the clear blue sky. Ha Ha Bay is another chasm. But few trees break the monotony of the crumbling hills, for a distance of some seventy miles between it and the wooded shores of the St. Lawrence.

The Class, on returning, took the direct steamer for Quebec. The water-way is full of the associations of song and story. We give here a legend of one of the islands.

THE PRISONER OF CRANE'S ISLAND.

"You have led a gay life, De Granville. Such a life unfits a man for devotion to his wife and family. I have lived in Paris, and have seen the tendency of the love of society. You certainly would not give up society for me."

The words were spoken by a high-born lady, famous for her beauty and accomplishments. She might have been a social queen. But her principles were Calvinistic, whatever may have been her church. She moved in social circles as one might pass through a boulevard on a fête day on a mission of duty. She had a high sense of duty that was as foreign to the feverish atmosphere of the French capital as the white edelweiss of the Alps to the flaming summer of the tropics.

"I will give up everything for you," replied the handsome young officer.

"But what proof have I that your fidelity to me will be greater than it has been to others for whom you have had a like regard and affection?"

"Proof? I will tell you. There lies on the St. Lawrence, in the newly settled regions of the west, a group of islands. They are lofty and lonely,— the home of the sea-birds, blazing with the reflected light of the sea in summer time, and eternally beautiful with evergreens, even amid the winter snows. They lie near Quebec, the capital of the France of the New World. I will go to the largest of these islands, and will there build a château. I will take you there, and we will there live alone, apart from the world; and I will only go when you bid me go, and come when you bid me come. Could a Christian knight offer more than this?"

About the year 1750 this young officer and his bride arrived at the picturesque little archipelago in the St. Lawrence, some thirty or more miles from Quebec, now known as Crane's Island. On the principal island, higher and more picturesque than the others, a château arose, and was furnished in the fine style of a French provincial residence of a century ago. De Granville had obtained from France the Seigneury of these romantic islands; and here, amid the sublime scenery of mountains, islands, and the river, he lived for a time in perfect happiness with his devoted and beautiful wife.

Madame de Granville was a woman of intense feelings, and such a nature is usually disturbed by jealousies. She was perfect in her devotion to her high-born husband's happiness; but she exacted a like devotion in return, and for a time received it.

THE SETTLERS AND INDIANS MERRY-MAKING.

These were happy years at the château. The two loved nature, and here was spread out before their eyes one of the most enchanting scenes in the New World. It was constantly changing; it varied with the year. Now the river was as pulseless as a mirror; now it was white with the foam of waves lashed by the storm; now it was golden in the sunrise; now the setting sun shone upon it and turned it into a red sea. The mountains, too, changed with the sky. The calm of summer, the splendors of autumn, the eternal whiteness of winter, — all were like sublime pictures and poems, and lent to the life in the château a perpetual charm.

VIEW IN THE THOUSAND ISLANDS.

The sea birds made their home on the islands, and were tame. In summer ships passed by, bearing the loved flag of the Fleur-de-lis.

Quebec had lost the influence of Champlain and his missionary associates. It was now a gay city, — a new Paris. The old times of restraint were gone. The settlements upon the beautiful river followed the customs of the queen city. There was a gay tone in the society of most of the provincial villages; and in the customary merry-makings the Indians united with the French.

De Granville began to mingle in the pleasantries of the mixed people on the river. He was pleased with the semi-barbarian chiefs, and the simplicity and beauty of the Indian maidens. He attended the Indians' feasts and danced with the daughters of the warriors.

In short, he came to love his evenings with the French fiddlers and the dusky people of the forest more than the severe society at the château.

He began to absent himself from his home so much that his beautiful young wife felt the neglect, and wondered what business could so often call him away.

"I am going hunting to-day," he would say in winter; and "I am going fishing to-day," in summer. His boat usually returned to the château late at night.

"What can keep the Seigneur so much away?" said Madame de Granville one day to an old servant.

The woman was silent.

"Have you any theory?"

"I have a suspicion."

"*A suspicion!*"

"The Indian maidens have bright eyes, and the *habitans* fiddle well."

De Granville was absent. It was a summer afternoon. Madame de Granville turned coldly away from her servant, and in an hour afterward was seen crossing the river in a boat.

The summer evenings on the St. Lawrence are rosy and long. In old times, after the toils of the day, the French had their pastimes, in which the Indians joined. There was a dance that night in the French and Indian village.

Just as De Granville was leading out a gayly attired Indian maiden, to the music of the fiddle, a dark, tall form appeared upon the clearing. The merry-making ceased. The shadow approached De Granville, whispered a single word to him, and led him away. The Indians fled, supposing that they had seen a spectre. The boat returned to the château in silence.

"Is this your fidelity?" said the proud lady as they landed. . "It seems that the society of Indians has become to you more than that of your wife. Are you ready to make a vow?"

"I will, if I can fulfil it. Name it."

"That you will never leave the island again."

"I will make the vow."

Years passed; the château was silent. What passed therein no one may know. But De Granville never crossed the St. Lawrence again; and when death had released him from his exile and imprisonment, Madame de Granville returned to her family in France, and the château crumbled into dust.

If the sunrise on the St. Lawrence floods the world from which the curtains of night are withdrawn with a peculiar brilliancy and splendor, the sunset is even more glorious. The river is usually calm, and the air clear. The west crimsons, the mid-heavens turn to gold, and a tremulous glory hangs over the mountains, woods, and waters. Dark shadows appear on the eastern slopes of the hills. The villages are like pictures. The sails on the ships hang loose in the breathless air. There is silence everywhere. The world seems to have settled into an eternal calm, as though Christ's feet had passed over the waters, and his lips had spoken again the Galilean word, " Peace."

CHAPTER XI.

QUEBEC.

UEL bee!"—"What a beak!"—exclaimed the old French voyagers, as, moving down the majestic St. Lawrence, they saw the rock that is now called Point Diamond. The cry of wonder has lived in the name of the city that occupies the most picturesque situation in America.

"There is not in the world a nobler outlook than from the Terrace at Quebec," said Sir Charles Dilke.

"Too much has not been said about the scenery of Quebec," wrote cynical Thoreau.

Had the wonder-working powers of the earth, air, and sea once met to fashion a place of harmonious and perfect beauty, the result might have been Quebec. It certainly has no equal in beauty in the New World; and Coblentz on the Rhine, which it resembles, is far less grand and beautiful.

The peculiar charm of Quebec lies in no particular point, but in a combination of the whole,—in the islands, mountains, rivers, cliffs, plains, waterfalls; in the quaintness of its buildings, in the associations of romance and history, and in the courteous simplicity of the people.

Stand upon the Terrace on a summer afternoon. Below you are the sag-roofed houses of the old French town. Was the like ever seen in America? Quaint dormer-windows, wooden bridges from roof

QUEBEC.

to roof, chimneys and coigns crowding against the rocks, narrow *rues* and queer churches.

Beyond is the resplendent St. Lawrence, with its ships and steamers idling in the sun. How calm and restful! Yet the great inland seas of Superior, Michigan, Huron, and Erie are pouring themselves through

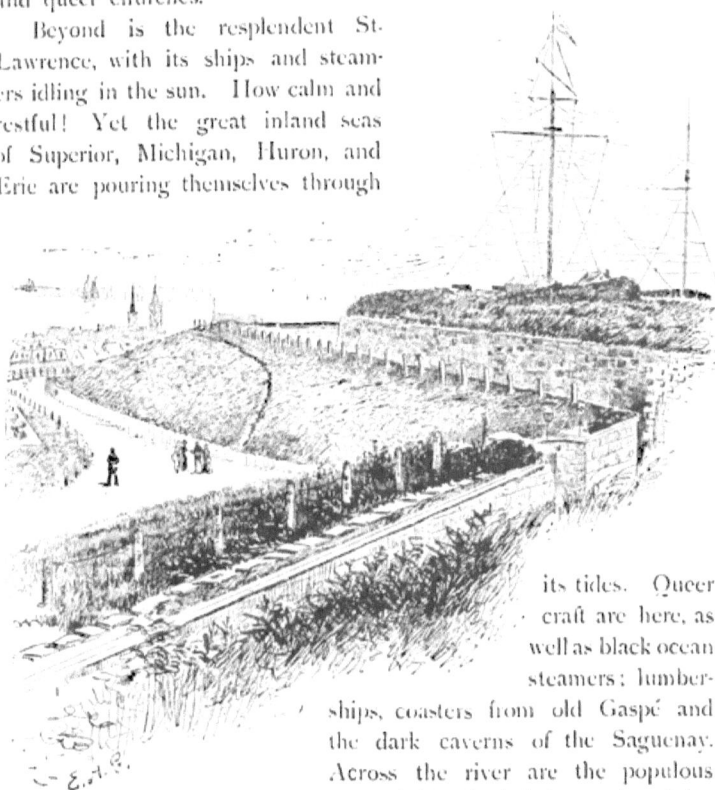

its tides. Queer craft are here, as well as black ocean steamers; lumber-ships, coasters from old Gaspé and the dark caverns of the Saguenay. Across the river are the populous heights of Point Levi, the vine-covered island of Orleans, the plains of the east with their Norman houses and churches. Mountains wall the sky, wearing the clouds like mantles. Behind you is the garden of the monument of Wolfe, and above you is the lofty and majestic castle, standing between earth and heaven, — a very monarch of the air, earth, and sea. It is the keeper of the St. Lawrence, — a grim giant, whose word is destiny.

What scenes have been enacted on the rocks and fields around you! Here was the Château of St. Louis, erected in the year of the "Mayflower," the palace of the French governors in provincial days. Here dwelt plumed chiefs; and hence their plumes departed into the setting sun. Grand was the Court of the old French deputies and knights. Their empire extended from the frozen North to the Gulf of Mexico. It was almost as great as all Europe, and combined all climates and resources. Here were enacted the heroic dramas of Montgomery, Arnold, Wolfe, and Montcalm. Here Champlain died on Christmas day; here stood for years the church that he had founded; here assembled the grandees to feast, and the missionaries to lay their plans for the conversion of the vast Indian world.

In the great churches and the establishments of learning and charity, choirs are heard singing. Bells ring; birds light upon the great guns pointing towards the sea, and flowers grow under the same instruments of death; while all is sunlight, calm, and peace. There is not another Quebec in all the world. Its earliest known history is a romance. Jacques Cartier came here from St. Malo in 1535. He beheld the beak-like rock darkening the air.

"What river is this?" he asked of the Indians.

"A river that has no end."

Here reigned King Donnacona. When Cartier returned from "the greatest river that is known ever to have been seen," he took Donnacona away with him. The barbarian king was baptized with great pomp in the great Cathedral of Rouen, and he died in France.

The romantic period of Champlain followed; of Henry IV.; of Richelieu and his Hundred Associates. Then came the times of Louis XIV., the "Grand Monarch." Frontenac here held a vice-regal Court. At times the Fleur-de-lis was lowered and the Red Cross

STREET IN QUEBEC.

of England floated over the castle; but under either flag Quebec
has always been a French city. She is Normandy to-day. One
need not go abroad, but only come here, to live in Europe and in the
Middle Ages.

The French King once sent over to the province a thousand
young women, most of them Nor-
mans, to become the wives of the settlers
of New France. The descendants of
these girls may be seen to-day in the
Market-place without the gates, as Norman as their great-grandmothers; as neat,
as pious, and as beautiful. There is no
scene more simple and charming in America than the long rows of French market-
girls on their carts of vegetables, fruits,
and flowers, with their patient little horses.
It is like a scene in a play.

JACQUES CARTIER.

Quebec is a city of churches, primitive piety, and simple virtues.
Said an old French missionary of the celestial atmosphere of the
old-time place, " To dwell in New France is to live in the bosom
of God." In the morning hours one may find the old churches
filled with worshippers, — men, women, boys, girls, on their way to
and from the markets. Faith here remains; the heaven is full of
angels; every one is on a journey to the regions of brighter hopes
and a larger and more perfected life.

The old Castle of St. Louis that Champlain founded is gone.
The beautiful Terrace is its memorial. What scenes took place
in its grand old Hall! What councils for the government of an
empire that once comprehended the whole American continent north
of the Great Lakes and the Gulf of Mexico!

The Class took lodgings in the old Albion Hotel. The boys
soon after their arrival visited the Terrace. It was evening. The

flags were floating from the airy pavilions; hundreds, perhaps thousands, of light-hearted people were on the long promenade, and below lay the St. Lawrence by moonlight, with an atmosphere of loneliness and mystery on the opposite shore.

In the morning they went outside of St. John's Gate with the landlord, and passed through the great Market in the open air.

CATHEDRAL.

They returned and visited the old sign of the Chien d'Or, or the Golden Dog, over the entrance of the old city post-office. In the afternoon Master Lewis related to them, on the Terrace, the dark tragedy associated with the sign, and advised them to read Kirby's romance, "Le Chien d'Or," saying that it was, in his opinion, one of the finest historical works in American fiction.

Charlie Leland first read the book, spending on it two days on the Terrace. He seemed like one in a dream. The other boys made excursions on these days to the Isle of Orleans and the Falls of Montmorency, but he did not wish to accompany them. When he had finished the book late on a summer evening, he said, —

"I am going to-morrow to see the Château Bigot."

"It is a ruin," said Master Lewis. "The book has interested you, as it?"

"Yes."

"I knew it would. I had another reason in commending the book to you. It not only relates a story as romantic as Fair Rosamond, but it clearly shows how the American empire was lost to France."

MARKET-PLACE, QUEBEC.

He added: " As long as Quebec maintained the virtues of Champlain, the power of France in America was as firm as the rock on which it was enthroned. When the deputies of France began to practise the vices of the corrupt Court of Louis XV., the French power weakened. Intendant Bigot, a weak, voluptuous, avaricious man,

THE PROMENADE AT QUEBEC.

prepared the way for the fall of the empire. I will go with you to-morrow to his once famous château."

The château is a massive ruin, some five miles from Quebec, at the foot of Charlesbourg Mountain. It is sometimes called the Hermitage, and frequently, by the French, the Mansion of the Mountain.

In the times of Bigot the palace, or château, was the seat of the Royal Government of France. It was almost the size of a small town. The buildings formed a square. They were surrounded by beautiful gardens. The St. Charles flowed by them. Beyond the parks and pavilions were the grounds of the Jesuits.

Francis Bigot, the last Intendant of the throne of France in Canada, was a native of Guienne. He received his appointment at the time of the universal corruption of French society and politics, — the days of Madame de Pompadour.

Who was Madame de Pompadour?

It sometimes happens that a young woman gifted with beauty, wit, talent, or musical ability is tempted to become untrue to her home, her family, and to herself for the sake of fame. But fame won at the expense of character never brings happiness, and by the inevitable laws of life ends always in regret.

Never did a woman gain so much power, wealth, and worldly splendor in return for an untrue life, as Madame de Pompadour. Her maiden name was Jeanne Antoinette Poisson. She was a girl of remarkable wit and beauty. She had dramatic power of a high order, was a brilliant musician and a lover of the fine arts. Many suitors sought her favor, and at an early age she married a wealthy man, — Le Normay l'Étioles. He loved her devotedly, and lived almost wholly for her happiness.

Her mother was an ambitious woman. Dissatisfied and scheming, she is said to have taunted her daughter with having married a banker when her beauty and her wit were worthy of a noble.

Fickle, unprincipled, and eager for position, Jeanne soon tired of her beautiful home and devoted husband, and resolved, if possible, to attract the attention of the king, Louis XV., who had inherited the wealth and glory of his father, the "Grand Monarch."

She placed herself before his carriage in the park, dressed in the most attractive manner, that she might be seen by the king. Dazzled by her beauty, he sought her out, invited her to his palace, and soon she became the mistress of Versailles. In vain her husband

MADAME DE POMPADOUR AND THE KING.

pleaded with her; she heartlessly abandoned him to become the favorite of a king.

Her ambition was gratified. Her influence with her royal lover became supreme. She made and dismissed ministers of state, created cardinals, declared war, and arranged terms of peace. The Council of State used to meet in her boudoir. She once declared that her very lap-dog was wearied with the fondlings of nobles. She virtually compelled Maria Theresa to address her as *ma cousine*, and a jest at her expense is said to have been the origin of the Seven Years' War. There were concerts, private theatricals, games, masques, constantly going on under her direction in the palace. She squandered enormous sums from the State Treasury in furnishing entertainments for the king.

The age of forty found her prematurely old, and with a corroding sense of unworthiness in her heart. She had had her will, and with what result? Listen to her own words: —

"What a situation is that of the great! They only live in the future, and are only happy in hope. There is no peace in ambition. I am always gloomy; the kindness of the king, the regards of courtiers, the attachment of domestics, affect me no longer. I have no more an inclination for all that once pleased me. My residence at Bellevue is charming, and I alone cannot endure it. I do not live; I am dead before my time. The public hatred grieves me exceedingly. My life is a *continued* death!"

She breathed her last amid the splendors of Versailles, at the age of forty-two.

The day of her burial was tempestuous. The king stood at the window of the palace as the funeral *cortège* moved away. He had long since tired of the woman who had violated conscience and God's laws for his favor, and now he looked with silent indifference on her burial car fading away in the storm. No love of husband or of child followed it; few tears were shed.

"The Marchioness has a rather wet day to set out on her long journey," the king jestingly said.

Long journey! The pomps of the palaces had faded; the illusion was done. She had sown to sin, had reaped its rewards, and in the pitiless rain they put away the form of Madame de Pompadour forever in a dishonored grave.

Little remains of the Intendant's palace, — a few gables, a few partition walls of immense thickness, and a few mounds. Birds build their nests there; red-alder trees grow over the crumbling masonry; the star-flower and Canadian violet sprinkle the sod; and mosses and tall grass cover the place of the fallen tower.

Bigot erected the palace as his country-seat. He here stored the public funds, and peculated from them. He here attempted to live the dissolute life that prevailed in the Court and among the nobles of France before the Revolution.

There were noble forests near the château. Bigot was fond of hunting, and he organized brilliant hunting-parties here.

One day, while hunting, he lost his way in a thick forest. Night came on. In his distress he chanced to meet an Indian girl. Her name was Caroline. She had French blood in her veins, and was very beautiful. He told her who he was, and said, —

"Caroline, show me the way to the castle."

She led him a long distance, and then pointed out to him the tower of the palace in the moonlight.

"Come with me to the castle, and I will reward you."

Caroline followed him. He gave her a place in the household.

Bigot was a married man. His wife was a high-born lady, passionate and jealous. She resided in Quebec, and did not often visit the château.

Bigot became enamored of the Indian maiden. He began to spend more time in her society than in that of his wife. Madame

Bigot noticed her husband's indifference towards her, but for a time she did not dream of the cause.

An old servant, who had learned something of the state of affairs at the château, one day ventured to hint to Madame Bigot that her husband had other motives than State interests in remaining so much away from Quebec.

" What? "

" Affection."

" For whom? "

" A beautiful Algonquin."

" Where? "

" At the château."

That evening a masked woman on horseback left Quebec. At midnight she quietly glided into the château. In the morning Caroline was found murdered in her room. By whom? No one knew. Only this; a disguised woman had been seen entering the château, and she had as mysteriously disappeared as she had come.

Caroline was buried in a cellar of the château, and a stone was placed over her, bearing the single letter " C."

Bigot robbed the province. He was at last arrested in France and sent into exile. His dissipated vice-regal Court at Quebec corrupted the society of the period; and his bad government caused the Lilies of France to be lowered from the great fortress of the West after they had waved above the St. Lawrence for a hundred and fifty years.

A ROMANCE THAT LOST AN EMPIRE.

In 1759 the famous expedition of General Wolfe and Admiral Saunders arrived in front of Quebec, which was under the command of the brave Montcalm. It was June. The troops were landed, and the city and fortress of Quebec were invested.

The summer passed; but the Gibraltar of the North, now impregnable, was like a knight clad in mail. The Lilies of France, in the red summer mornings and evenings, waved peacefully over the Fortress of St. Louis, as though the fifty vessels of war, the fifteen thousand sailors, and nine thousand soldiers were a thousand miles away.

September came. The English commanders had the conviction that the capture of the fortress was impossible, and the sailors and soldiers were losing all confidence in the success of the expedition.

MONTCALM.

One September night, beautiful as all nights of the September moons are on the St. Lawrence, General Wolfe and Admiral Saunders held a consultation on board of the flag-ship.

"Some new plan must be adopted, or the siege abandoned," was in substance the conclusion of each.

A petty officer entered, and handed a communication to General Wolfe. It was marked *Private and Important.*

The General opened it, and said to the Admiral,

"Here is a curious communication from a Captain Robert Stobo, of Halifax. He was once, he claims, detained at Quebec as a hostage, having been made a prisoner of war by the French. He has information that he deems important, which he wishes to communicate."

"Where is he now?"

"On board the vessel."

"Let us listen to him."

A person of fine appearance was admitted.

He was courteously received.

"Well, Captain, what have you to say?" asked General Wolfe.

"For a number of months I was a resident of Quebec, a prisoner on parole. My life was a lonely one for a time, but I at last became acquainted with a beautiful French lady, of high social position, and we became deeply attached to each other. We used to meet and walk upon the Heights of Abraham, and she made known

THE PLAINS OF ABRAHAM.

to me a secret path that leads from the Plains of Abraham to the river. It is the only path that can be followed up and down the Heights. An army could ascend the Heights by it at night, marching in single file. I have come from Halifax to put you in possession of my chart of the Heights and of this secret path."

General Wolfe took the chart, and with the Admiral examined the Lovers' Path.

The captain was dismissed with expressions of gratitude. All that night the two officers studied the defile that the beautiful French *habitant* had disclosed to her lover.

"Admiral," said General Wolfe, at last, "I am disposed to try it."

It was the night of September 12, described as glorious by the old chroniclers. General Wolfe passed from vessel to vessel, and addressed his men.

The Lovers' Path, like a picture, was impressed on his mind as in a dream

> " 'The paths of glory lead but to the grave,' "

he said; and added, "I would rather be the author of that one poem, Gray's Elegy, than gain the glory of defeating the French to-morrow."

The oars beat the swiftly flowing tide. The Heights darkened the air above. Wolfe gazed upward. He repeated : —

> " 'The boast of heraldry, the pomp of power,
>   And all that beauty, all that wealth, e'er gave,
>   Await alike the inevitable hour.
>   The paths of glory lead but to the grave.' "

At one o'clock on the morning of the 13th, Wolfe led his silent army, marching in single file, up the Lovers' Path.

The result is told in history, in pictures, and in monumental works of art.

But the path of glory brought to Wolfe his "inevitable hour." Leading the charge, he was three times wounded.

"Support me," he said. "Let them not see me drop."

They brought him water.

"They flee," said the officer on whose breast he was leaning.

"Who?" asked the dying man.

"The enemy."

"God be praised, — I die happy."

The elaborate and heroic monument to Wolfe in Westminster Abbey, and the tall shaft to his memory in the garden of the Terrace of Quebec, can hardly fail to recall Gray's pensive reflections in connection with the splendid achievement that gave to England an empire as large as Europe, and that made him immortal.

Stobo was rewarded by New England with one thousand dollars and by honors from the Crown. But the Frenchwoman's name was never known.

"MARCHE DONC!"

The Canadian *calèche*, like a London hansom, is a somewhat peculiar vehicle. It is usually a rather shabby and rickety two-wheeled carriage; and these adjectives would not apply to the hansom, which is usually substantial and elegant. The driver does not sit at the back, but on a narrow seat in front of the passengers.

DEATH OF WOLFE.

Charlie Leland and Charlie Noble, seeing the queer vehicle in the streets, asked Master Lewis to engage one for them to take them to the Falls. Master Lewis intrusted the matter to the landlord, who advised them to take some other carriage.

" Why do you want a calèche ? " he asked.

" It looks so picturesque," said Noble.

" Antiquated, he means," said Leland.

" Provincial," corrected Leland.

As beautiful as Quebec itself is, are its surrounding villages. As

CALÈCHE.

one who has not seen her suburbs has not seen Boston, so one who has not seen the country around Quebec has seen but half the capital.

The driver seemed a very silent man. Down Palace Street moved the vehicle, and past the church of St. Roch. The road was broad and firm. The little horse trotted along easily, and Beauport was soon gained, and the church, with its lofty spires, left behind. Quaint stone houses, whitewashed, and surrounded with beds of flowers, lined the road. Nearly all the people are of French origin.

A noble estate was reached, beautiful in its situation, and having an air of dignity and antiquity.

"To whom do these grounds belong?" asked Charlie Leland of the driver.

The man bowed and smiled, and said, "Marche donc!"

"Marshal Donc," said Charlie to Charlie.

They came to Huldimand House. Stopping here, they chanced to hear a gentleman say that this house was once occupied by the father of the queen.

"Who was the father of the queen?" asked Charlie of Charlie.

"I do not know. I think it was George III. Let us ask the driver."

"Who was the father of Queen Victoria?" asked Noble.

The driver bowed and smiled, and said, "Marche donc!"

"Marshal Donc," said Charlie to Charlie. "I never understood the succession. I knew that there was a break somewhere. Marshal Donc was probably one of the sons of George III. He had a great family; and the Prince of Wales died, you know."

The Falls were lovely this dreamy summer afternoon. They looked like a crystal river suspended in the air. The boys had enjoyed their ride so much that they wished to continue it.

"Somewhere else," said Leland to the driver.

He did not seem to comprehend.

"It is all beautiful, — anywhere," said Charlie Noble.

The driver seemed puzzled.

"Église," said Leland.

The driver bowed and said, "Marche donc!"

"The church of Marshal Donc," said Charlie to Charlie.

The road lay over sunny hills. It was lined with small houses, large barns, and bright gardens. Here and there were shrines.

At a distance of some fifteen or more miles from Quebec, the driver stopped before an ancient classic church. It was built of gray stone.

The boys entered the church. It was full of pictures, and along the cornices and in the

ST. ANNE'S CHURCH.

sacristy were great piles of crutches. There were many invalids in the church, praying.

"What church is this?" asked Charlie Leland of an English gentleman, whom he met before a picture of a storm at sea.

"St. Anne."

" I thought it was the church of Marshal Donc. May I ask what is the meaning of all these crutches?"

" They have been left by the people who have been cured."

" How extraordinary!" said Charlie. " Who is St. Anne?"

"She was the mother of the Virgin."

" But how does she heal cripples?"

" A part of her body is here, — some of her bones. The relics are shown at Mass. This is a miracle-church. Nearly a hundred thousand people visit it every year."

The little horse began to scamper when his head was turned again towards Quebec. The driver seemed to the boys to be meditating on departed greatness, he so frequently said, " Marche donc!"

As Quebec appeared in view, like a city climbing up the heights to the castle, the view was wonderful. The windows blazed in the setting sun, and the metal roofs shone like silver.

" Who was Marshal Donc?" asked Charlie Leland of the landlord, as he came into the hotel near midnight. " The driver kept speaking about him on the way, — the father of the queen, I think he said."

" Oh, — *Go along!*"

" The landlord is not very polite to-night," said Charlie to Charlie. " Let us retire."

On one of the rides from Quebec a friend of Master Lewis related to the boys an amusing incident he had read, and which was suggested by an occurrence on the way. The road was hot and dusty, and a French emigrant hung his bundle on the back of the carriage. " A German emigrant," said he, " once ran up behind an elegant carriage, and hung his boots, which he was carrying in his hand, over one of the braces. Presently the driver, not knowing what the man had done, put whip to the horses, and left the bootless traveller behind.

" An elegantly attired lady was the sole occupant of the carriage. The German ran, calling out lustily to the driver to stop.

" The lady, hearing the call, looked behind. She saw a man running after the carriage, swinging aloft his arms and shouting to the driver.

" She was a very imaginative and nervous lady, and she ordered the driver to run the horses, and began to scream hysterically.

" The carriage flew. The poor emigrant saw his boots disappearing with a suddenness and velocity that filled him with rage and despair.

"But shortly, greatly to his amazement and delight, an accident happened to the vehicle. One of the wheels came off.

"The man redoubled his speed. When the lady saw him coming, she fell down on the floor of the half-overturned carriage and began to beg for mercy.

"Her prayer was answered. The German came up, panting for breath, seized his boots and merely said, 'Thank Heaven! I'm in luck!'

"Without a word to the driver or lady, he wiped the sweat from his face, and went joyfully on his way."

The gentleman entertained the Class with some pleasant illustrations of this story in a German paper, and was careful that the French traveller did not meet with any such episode with his bundle.

The Class spent many evenings on the Terrace. The boys, following the suggestion of Master Lewis, made a study of Mackay's "Songs of Emigration." They practised them daily in one of the airy pavilions on the Terrace. One of the songs,

"Cheer, boys, cheer; the merry breeze is blowing,"

always attracted the attention and stopped the feet of the passing throngs.

CUSTOM HOUSE, QUEBEC.

The evenings on the Terrace were delightful. The castle seemed to be built up into the sunset air. The St. Lawrence flowed calmly by. Great steamers went out of the port and came into it. Hundreds of emigrants landed at Point Levi, from all the dark steamers that came in from Liverpool.

QUEBEC.

Quebec is the monument of Champlain. It is worthy of its founder, whose virtues will lend to it the light of their influence forever, whatever may be its changes, or whatever flag may float above the fortress. Virtues shine like the stars.

THE STAR IN THE WEST.

QUEBEC, 1635.

'Tis the Fortress of St. Louis,
　The Church of Recoverance;
And hang o'er the crystal Crosses
　The silver Lilies of France.
In the fortress a knight lies dying,
　In the church are priests at prayer,
And the bell of the Angelus sweetly
　Throbs out on the crimsoned air.

The noblest knight is dying
　That ever served a king;
And he looks from the fortress window
　As the bells of the Angelus ring.
Old scenes come back to his vision;
　Again his ship's canvases swell
In the harbor of gray St. Malo,
　In the haven of fair Rochelle.
He sees the imparadised ocean
　That he dared when his years were young;
The lagoons where his lateen sail drifted
　As the Southern Cross over it hung;
Acadie; the Richelieu's waters;
　The lakes through the midlands that rolled;
And the Cross that he planted wherever
　He lifted the Lilies of gold.
He lists to the Angelus ringing,
　He folds his white hands on his breast;
And, lo! o'er the pine-clouded forests
　A Star verges low in the West! —

I.

" Star on the bosom of the West —
　Chime on, O bell, chime on, O bell! —
To-night with visions I am blest,
　And filled with light ineffable!
No angels sing in crystal air,
　No clouds 'neath seraphs' footsteps glow,
No feet of seers o'er mountains fair
　A portent follows far; but, lo!

A Star is glowing in the West :
　The world shall follow it from far.
Chime on, O Christmas bells, chime on !
　Shine on, shine on, O Western Star !

II.

" In yonder church that storms have iced —
　I founded it upon this rock —
I 've daily kissed the feet of Christ,
　In worship with my little flock.
But I am dying, — I depart ;
　Like Simeon old, my glad feet go.
A star is shining in my heart
　Such as the Magi saw ; and, lo !
　　A Star is shining in the West :
　　　The world shall hail it from afar.
　　Chime on, O Christmas bells, chime on !
　　　Shine on, shine on, O Western Star !

III.

" Beside the Fleur-de-lis of France,
　The faith I 've planted in the North.
Ye messengers of Heaven, advance ;
　Ye mysteries of the Cross, shine forth !
I know the value of the earth ;
　I 've learned its lessons ; it is done :
One soul alone outweighs in worth
　The fairest kingdom of the sun.
　　Star on the bosom of the West,
　　　My dim eyes follow thee afar.
　　Chime on, chime on, O Christmas bells !
　　　Shine on, shine on, O golden Star !

IV.

" What rapture ! hear the sweet choirs sing !
　While death's cold shadows o'er me fall,
Beneath the Lilies of my King,
　Go, light the lamps in yonder hall !
Mine eyes have seen the Christ-Star glow
　Above the New World's temple gates.
Go forth, celestial heralds, go !
　Earth's fairest empire thee awaits !
　　Star on the bosom of the West,
　　　What feet shall follow thee from far !
　　Chime on, O Christmas bells, chime on !
　　　Shine on forever, golden Star ! "

'T was Christmas morn ; the sun arose
  'Mid clouds o'er the St. Lawrence broad.
And fell a sprinkling of the snows
  As from the uplifted hand of God.
Dead in the fortress lay the knight,
  His white hands crossed upon his breast, —
Dead, he whose clear prophetic sight
  Beheld the Christ-Star in the West.
That morning, 'mid the turrets white,
  The low flags told the empire's loss :
They hung the Lilies o'er the knight,
  And by the Lilies set the Cross.

Long on Quebec's immortal heights
  Has Champlain slept, the knight of God.
The Western Star shines on, and lights
  The growing empires, fair and broad.
And though are gone the knights of France,
  Still lives the spirit of the North ;
The heralds of the Star advance,
  And Truth's eternal light shines forth.

CHAPTER XII.

 HAVE heard celestial voices," said a pious publican of Anjou to a priest of Paris.

"So have I, and I have had a vision of the Virgin and the Saviour," said the priest.

"What did the angels say to you?" continued the priest.

"They bade me establish a new mission — in the West — on the St. Lawrence; it may be in that beautiful island that Cartier discovered nearly a hundred years ago."

"How wonderful!" said the priest. "The voices I heard and the visions I have seen have given me the same direction. We must unite for this work. Let us proclaim our calling, and see what the Church will do to aid us."

The two soon met again.

"The Saviour has appeared to me," said the priest.

"The Virgin has shown herself to me in a vision," said the publican.

"'T is the isle of Mont Royal."

"Yes, the isle of Mont Royal."

The two told their visions to priests and nobles. The nobles favored the mission, and gave the two missionaries the means to purchase the isle of Montreal.

18

The two, after these real impressions or supposed visions, were full of zeal for mission work in the wilderness of the West. They formed the society of Notre Dame de Montreal.

There was a thrilling missionary service in the grand Cathedral of Notre Dame in Paris in February, 1641. The Lord of Maisonneuve and forty-five noble associates consecrated to the work of God the great island of the Upper St. Lawrence under the name of Ville Marie de Montreal.

The ships sailed. On May 18, 1642, Lord Maisonneuve and his mission colony landed at the fort of Montreal.

He immediately erected an altar. It was the beautiful month of May. The trees were bursting into green leaves; flowers were nestling among the grass; birds were singing in the trees. Primeval forests covered Montreal; the rapids foamed afar, and the broad St. Lawrence flowed calmly by on its way from the great lakes to the gulf and the ocean.

Mass was said before the newly erected Cross. Then the priest uttered a prophecy: —

"You are a grain of mustard seed. The seed will spring up and grow; it will overshadow the land. You are few, but your work is the mission of God. His smile rests upon you; your children shall occupy the land."

Nearly two hundred and fifty years have passed. The isle of Montreal contains some two hundred thousand inhabitants. The city of Montreal is called the Queen of the St. Lawrence. The Hôtel Dieu and the school that those old missionaries founded still live.

Why, when so many other missions have failed and perished?

The mission was founded in the spirit of peace, and not in that spirit of conquest that spills the blood of men. It was founded in the spirit of charity, and was kept unstained from the crimes of bigotry. It outstretched its hand to meet the wants of men.

MONTREAL.

So beautiful has been the history of Montreal that one could wish to believe that the visions of the old French mystics were something more than the day-dreams of a benevolent heart and mind.

We relate the story as it was believed, and have no criticism to make upon it. Few cities in the world have had a more interesting beginning. The seeds of Montreal were Christian love. They sprang up, budded, and blossomed.

Victoria Square is not the Terrace of Quebec, and the fine hall of the Young Men's Christian Association is not the airy pavilions of the French city's promenade; but Mount Royal is a glorious eminence, and the view of the two great rivers, the mountains, and the city from the summit is one of the finest in America.

The Class made their first visit in the city to the Cathedral of Notre Dame, or the French Cathedral. It is perhaps the most interesting Catholic church in America. It holds ten thousand persons; in it marriages and funerals are constantly taking place, and occasionally both at the same time. The music is most impressive and often dramatic, and the great bell in one of its towers is the largest in America, weighing some fifteen tons.

The Songs of Emigration had interested the Class in that subject that tourists amid these lovely and enchanting scenes so little notice, — the pioneers of the New West. The vast Western Empire is yet to be the centre of the American world, and the tides of the Old World's populations are silently flowing into it. The men and women of its future development and greatness are not to be found in the faded châteaus of France or Quebec, or on the grand old English estates. They come in the steerages of the black ocean steamers, and the cabin passengers in the princely saloons are hardly aware of their presence on board.

The loiterers on the Terrace of Quebec see the steamers land across the river. Tugs take the cabin passengers to the city, perhaps a hundred in number, and carriages meet them and convey them to the fine hotels. An hour or two passes; then a thousand men, women, and children go over the plank, and wait the making up of a long emigrant train for the West. They are housed in sheds. The train makes up; it moves away for Ontario, Manitoba, the Georgian Bay.

What does it carry with it? "Only emigrants"? So the idlers say. It carries the heart, brain, and muscle of a rising empire. It carries people that are people, and not mere pensioners and tax-gatherers. The kings of the future are in it; the Queens, the princes. It separates rising families from decaying families,— the new from the old. It leaves oblivion behind; it enters life.

The disregarded emigrant is the founder of new cities, new churches, new schools. His industry is a mine; his faith is a crown; his children are to inherit the empire to come.

The Class found nothing among the grand public buildings and places that more interested them than a plain monument of stone, erected to the "memory of six thousand emigrants" who died of ship-fever in the emigrant sheds of Montreal. The monument was erected by the workmen on the Victoria Bridge.

Six thousand emigrants buried in one small lot, as it were in one grave! Guide-books do not mention them; histories give the fact a line; tourists pass hastily by to visit fine churches and halls. Six thousand! What pain, what misery without human sympathy, what partings in families, what disappointed hopes!

Blessed be the hands of those workmen whose hearts remembered the poor, and who placed the memorial over the six thousand in that one grave!

Montreal is a city of churches. Each of the leading denominations of Christians has at least one noble church edifice here.

It is an interesting experience to an American citizen to go to church in Canada. Within the compass of a few miles, in some

MARKET-PLACE OF BONSECOURS.

portions of the Dominion, the traveller can attend mass in a French
Catholic chapel in the early morning, the Anglican service at eleven

THE BANK OF MONTREAL.

o'clock, the Scotch Kirk in the afternoon, and the Methodist Church
in the evening.

But this is not all. He sees each of these services conducted
in its primitive and uncompromising force.

In the United States all that we derive from the Old World becomes quickly modified. There is something in our air that subdues and softens whatever is most peculiar and character-istic.

Thus a party of emigrants land in New York, clad in the durable but uncouth costume of their country and class; but in a few days the honest old clothes have begun to be discarded. Almost un-consciously both men and women have yielded to the dread of being peculiar, which is among the strongest feelings of our na-ture. Soon they secretly flatter themselves that no one would take them for foreigners.

Religion, being the chief conservative influence of the world, is slowest to submit to the modifying power of the new land. But the process goes on unceasingly. We can easily perceive that even the French Catholic of Canada is somewhat different from the French Catholic of New York or Boston.

We have seen in front of the old Cathedral of Montreal a mis-sionary-box inviting the contributions of the faithful. On the outside of the box were wax figures of hogs devouring priests and monks, and underneath was a sentence intimating that such was often the fate of devoted missionaries to the heathen.

It is safe to say that in no city of the United States would such an exhibition be ventured.

The interiors of many Catholic churches of Canada differ in nothing from those of village churches in the remoter provinces of France. The same kind of votive offerings hang at the shrines, and there is the same homely directness in the remarks of the curé, which startles the ears of Protestant visitors to the Departments of Southern France.

The most interesting experience of this kind is enjoyed in the Scotch Presbyterian kirks of New Brunswick and Nova Scotia. To attend one of these illuminates for us the whole history of Scotland

CATHEDRAL OF MONTREAL.

since the Reformation. It is a chapter of Sir Walter Scott come to life.

We vividly discern the secret of the hold which the religion of Knox and Calvin had upon the Covenanters and their children; for we see the kirk service performed in very much of its original amplitude and heartiness. Only one thing appears to be curtailed, and that is the sermon, now reduced to a reasonable length. All the rest appears unchanged.

There is the prim, unpainted, uncarpeted, straight-backed, utterly unattractive and comfortless interior, including the high gallery, the higher pulpit, the sounding-board, the elevated front seat for the choir, and the great square pews.

There is no shirking or compromise anywhere: (1) singing, in which every worshipper joins heartily, standing, — from the minister in the pulpit to the little children in the pew-corners; (2) Old Testament reading; (3) prayer, the congregation all standing; (4) singing again, every worshipper standing; (5) New Testament lesson; (6) prayer again; (7) singing; (8) sermon; (9) singing; (10) prayer; (11) collection; (12) notices; (13) singing; (14) benediction.

The most obvious difference between this service and that of our churches is the greater amount of bodily exertion put forth by the whole congregation. At every singing and during every prayer the people all stand. The singing is done with an energetic unanimity rarely heard in our cushioned and carpeted parlor-churches, wherein, for the most part, the congregation sits passive, in luxurious ease, from beginning to end.

The Class sang for the Young Men's Christian Association and in two of the charitable institutions. The boys here introduced Mackay's Songs of Emigration, and rendered "Cheer, boys, cheer," and "To the West! to the West!" with so much spirit and feeling as to win popular favor at the Association rooms, and a concert was asked for before it was offered. The hall was filled on the occa-

sion; the songs of America were well received, but the songs of the
Emigrants and the West were demanded again and again.

Charlie Noble was put into excellent spirits by the generous temper of the audience, and here gave another illustration of the admir-
able tact at his command when he was himself in a happy mood.

MONTREAL.

The audience encored "Cheer, boys, cheer," twice. On the second recall Charlie brought upon the platform an English and an
American flag, and used them both in conducting; clasping the
staffs together and intermingling the bunting in the stirring chorus.
The act called forth long and hearty applause.

The Class made an excursion from Montreal to Ottawa, and

THE WHARVES OF MONTREAL.

visited the noble Government buildings. The season, and the little interest taken in the matter by those to whom the subject was introduced, did not seem to promise well for a concert, and the Class returned to Montreal by the railroad to Lachine and by steamer down the Lachine Rapids. The tour was the means of adding to their programme Tom Moore's "Canadian Boat-Song," and the romantic and delightful old provincial river melody, —

> " Fringue ! fringue sur la rivière !
> Fringue ! fringue sur l'aviron ! "

The ballad relates how that the king's son went hunting with a silver gun ; how he aimed the silver gun at a black duck, but shot a white one, out of whose eyes came diamonds and out of whose mouth came silver. The melody is peculiarly charming. The story and music are alike mysterious in their origin.

THE BELL OF CAUGHNAWAGA.

Nine miles above Montreal, on the river St. Lawrence, is a quiet Indian village where lives the remnant of the old tribe of Caughnawagas.

The houses of the village are simple, but in their midst stands a massive stone church, colored by time. In the tower of the church hang two bells. One of these has a most remarkable history.

Near the close of the first century of colonization Father Nichols, a Catholic missionary, induced the Christian Indians of the then great nation of the Caughnawagas to put aside a certain portion of their game and furs for the purpose of purchasing a bell for his mission church. The Indians had never seen or heard a church bell ; but they were generous in meeting the appeal, and the bell was ordered from France.

The priest and the contributors waited long and patiently for the arrival of the bell, but it did not come. At length news reached Montreal that the French ship on which the bell had been placed had been captured by an English cruiser, and that the bell had been taken to the port of Salem, Massachusetts, and hung up in the belfry of the church at Deerfield, near that port.

INDIANS OF THE NORTH.

The Indians had looked for the coming of the bell like the advent of a god. They were greatly disappointed at its capture. Some of them said, — "Our warriors will one day bring hither the bell. The bell is the Lord's."

In 1704 the Marquis de Vaudreuil planned a hostile expedition against the New England colonies. He said to Father Nichols, —

"I must have the aid of the Caughnawagas."

"I will lead them myself, but on one condition."

"Name it."

INDIAN WARRIOR.

"That you will recapture the bell in the town of Deerfield, and allow us to bring it to Caughnawaga."

"You shall have your wish. I will order the commander to recover the bell."

Father Nichols assembled the Indians, and preached to them a crusade for the rescue of the bell.

His words were like fuel to a fire already kindled.

"The bell! the bell!" shouted the red crusaders. The idol of brass was to them as the Holy Sepulchre to the Knights of the Middle Ages, and they were impatient, if not to fight the battles of the Lord who had forbidden the shedding of blood, at least to fight in his name.

The expedition entered the English colonies in midwinter. It was a long and perilous march, and the French troops suffered and complained. The French soldiers knew that they were engaged merely in a war of conquest, and winter chilled the romance of such an expedition.

Not so with the Indian warriors. Father Nichols uplifted the banner of the Cross, and a convert bore it before them through the evergreens and over the white wastes of snow, and they advanced on their snow-shoes as though they had received the commissions of Heaven. Their watchword was "The bell! the bell!"

On the 29th of February Deerfield rose in sight over the fields of snow, — the Jerusalem of the red crusaders.

Early in the morning of the 1st of March, in the midst of a storm of high wind and driving snow, the army fell upon the town. The people of Deerfield could hardly have been more taken by surprise had an army descended from the clouds. An attack by the French and Indians in the winter was unlooked for by even the military towns of the colonies; but Deerfield, — what could have brought such an army here?

The Indians fell upon the people, and a fearful slaughter followed. The snow was crimsoned with blood. Forty-seven persons were killed, and one hundred and twenty were made prisoners. After the first flush of the barbaric triumph, the Indian warriors, with their hands red with gore, cried, "The bell! the bell!"

Father Nichols led them to the church, and said to a French soldier, "Go up and ring it."

The bell rung out over the reddened snow in the crystal air in which the storm of the morning was clearing.

The Indians listened with awe. They dropped upon their knees and uplifted their bloody hands in thanksgiving. Well, well, it was strange. *Te Deums* have been sung in Christian lands over deeds as dark as this; but towering above all such scenes as these, the Sermon on the Mount lives, and will live until all deeds of blood are remembered only as barbarisms, however they may have been lauded.

The bell was placed on poles, and borne in triumph towards Montreal. But the winter snows were yet deep, and March was pitiless, and Father Nichols

THE INDIANS ATTACKING THE SETTLERS.

allowed the bell to be buried near the frontier, at a place to which it would be safe to return for it in the late spring.

In the season of the birds and flowers and tender leaves, Father Nichols again led an expedition for the recovery of the bell. Canada awaited the return of the priest and his warriors.

The expedition came back in triumph. The Cross advanced out of the forest. Behind it were two white oxen bearing the bell on their yoke. The oxen and bell were garlanded with the flowers of spring.

The bell was brought to Caughnawaga, and hung up in the belfry of the Mission Church. A festival of rejoicing followed; and for years whenever the music of the bell was heard, the Indians dropped on their knees in prayer.

The bell still hangs in the old tower above the St. Lawrence. But its voice is not often heard, and it long ago ceased to be regarded as the voice of a god.

CHAPTER XIII.

TORONTO.

ORONTO, the city of Lake Ontario, is one of the surprises of the century. Its history is comprised in less than a century, yet it is a city of domes and spires, a city that has leaped into life, and is out-stripping the older cities in enterprise, progress, and industrial skill. The face of Toronto is turned towards the future; Montreal and Quebec look back towards the past.

The lake harbor of Toronto is serene and beautiful, and is often crowded with vessels and steamers. Toronto is the Liverpool of the lake. On one side of the city flows the river Don, and on the other side the Humber.

Toronto was founded by Governor Simcoe, of romantic history. The governor built a château on the Don. He was very hospitable; the Indians named him "One-whose-door-is-always-open." His son was one of those who fell in the breach at Badajos, Spain. His monument may be seen in the ancient cathedral at Exeter, England. The château is gone, and its site is a pleasure-ground.

The Esplanade, an embankment faced with masonry and over-looking the lake, is the principal pleasure-resort in summer. The Union Railway Station, whose high towers give it at a little distance the appearance of a castle, rises from the Esplanade.

Happy Canada! — *Canada felix!* — such is the name given to this grain-growing region in the West. Rugged and prosperous, of iron character and faith, proud, virtuous, and loving, the people form one of those noble communities that are the glory and strength of a country.

THOUSAND ISLANDS — ENTRANCE TO LAKE ONTARIO.

The French and Scottish families in this rich agricultural region maintain their provincialisms. The Scottish MacNabs and other Scottish families used to live after the manners and customs of Highland feudalism, and old Scotland may be found in some of the towns of Ontario to-day.

The MacNabs used to visit Toronto in blue bonnets and bright plaids. It is related that once when the old chief of this clan visited Kingston, he registered his name as "*The* MacNab."

A kinsman, on registering his name, wrote, "The *other* MacNab!"

We do not doubt that there were still *other* MacNabs; for the world is large, and *the* people are everywhere to be found as seen in their own imaginations. How happy many souls would be but for the *other* MacNab!

PARLIAMENT BUILDINGS, OTTAWA.

The "other MacNab" became famous. During the Canadian rebellion, when an army from the forest towns marched against Toronto, he defeated the insurgents with a force of a thousand volunteers.

The literary life of Toronto and its connecting towns is among the healthiest and best in Canada. Here lived the accomplished

Mrs. Jameson. Here have lived some of the most cultured French and Scottish families,— political refugees whose philosophy was too advanced for their times, and conservatives whom their times had outgrown. King's Street is stately with public buildings. Clubs and societies abound, and exert a marked intellectual influence. Toronto is a university town, and its colleges are noble buildings and occupy beautiful grounds. There are upwards of seventy churches in the city.

Ontario, of which Toronto is the capital, is very much larger than either Great Britain or Italy. In less than a hundred years its population has grown from two thousand to two million people.

A pamphlet published in the interests of English immigration thus speaks of this great province, which is destined to gather to itself an immense population, and perhaps become the most important part of the British Empire of the West: "The Province of Ontario is not only, from its position, resources, and water-power, likely to continue to be the workshop for the manufacturers of the Dominion, but it possesses a climate superior to that of any other Canadian province, and not inferior to the most favored climates in America. It extends from south to north over a distance of seven hundred miles, or from the parallel of forty-two degrees — that of Rome — to the parallel of fifty-two degrees on James Bay, a latitude still south of that of Birmingham. From near the mouth of the Ottawa in the east to the Lake of the Woods in the west it measures a length of nearly 1,100 miles. The area embraced within its very irregular boundaries is about 200,000 square miles, — a territory 80,000 square miles larger than the United Kingdom, 1,700 square miles larger than France, equal to the combined areas of Holland, Belgium, Switzerland, Portugal, and Italy, and only 12,000 square miles smaller than the whole German Empire." To this immense territory, 80,000 square miles larger than the United Kingdom, England has been sending her overcrowded population for a number of years,

Here the English emigrant finds himself no longer a tenant, but the master of his own home and lands.

Outside of the great depot at Toronto the Class saw a group of emigrants sitting on the ground, waiting for the making up of a train. Among them was a little baby, lying on the grass and smiling in the sun.

"Smile on!" one might say; "you have reason to smile. Your parents are heroic, and they have brought you to the land of promise. For you they came; that their children might have a larger, freer, and more hopeful life. Little one, smile on! The sun is setting, but it is the sun of the Western World."

The child of the English laborer may have hardships, but he can stand at the door of his cabin in Ontario and look towards the future with hope. Fate here has not decreed that he shall be dependent and poor.

England is famous for the striking contrast seen between the condition of its richest and that of its poorest classes. A very few Englishmen, compared with the population, own a large portion of the acres of the island; on the other hand, the country swarms with multitudes of people who are desperately poor and who are always on the very edge of beggary.

The laws and customs of England have always tended to gather the wealth of the land into a few great families. The old law of the primogeniture, which means the inheritance of the whole estate by the eldest son of a family to the exclusion of his brothers and sisters, largely aided in effecting this result; and the law of entail, which means the right of a proprietor to tie up his estate for many years, enabling him to dictate his successors for several generations, has still farther favored the accumulation of riches in the hands of a few.

Some facts as to the very rich, on the one hand, and the very poor, on the other, will show in bold relief how startling is the contrast.

Let us first take some of the rich men and see how vast are their possessions. One quarter of the whole kingdom of Scotland, for instance, is owned by eight noblemen. It is said that the Duke of Sutherland can ride from sunrise to sunset without seeing any land but his own out of the carriage window; and he has five lordly castles. Nearly the whole county of East Sussex is included in the estates of two men, the Duke of Richmond and Lord Laconfield. The young Marquis of Bute owns almost all the flourishing and busy town of Cardiff, and many of the coal mines in its vicinity; his income is over a million dollars a year, and his principal residence, Crichton Mount Stuart, is so vast that it recently cost the marquis nearly two millions of dollars to put it in repair.

The property of some great noblemen in London is enormous. There is the Duke of Westminster, who owns Eaton and Belgrave Squares, two of the finest and most fashionable squares in the city; besides many streets entirely composed of blocks of elegant and luxurious houses in the heart of Westminster, where land costs hundreds of dollars a foot. Besides this immense London property, the duke has three noble castles in the country, around which are many thousands of rich acres and beautiful parks of which he is lord and master.

The Duke of Bedford also has very large possessions in the very centre of London, including half a dozen squares, Covent Garden Theatre and Market, and long rows of houses on main streets, like the Strand and Great Russell Street. The Duke of Devonshire, besides many London houses, has eight castles and palaces in the country, each of which he maintains, with retinues of servants, all the year round.

Let us glance now at the very poor. John Bright says there are a million paupers living on the parishes in England, and another million who are all the time on the verge of beggary.

The poor peasants in the southern shires, who toil from earliest dawn until kindly darkness comes to relieve them of light and so of work, get only three or four dollars a week, and live in miserable, broken-down, dirty huts, where the rain leaks in and the cold blasts sweep through remorselessly.

These peasants are often crowded six or eight together in a single miserable little room; even the cheap blessing of pure water is often beyond their reach, and they live in a state of squalor which breeds disease and death. Many of them seldom taste meat from one year's end to another, but live on wheaten cakes and potatoes; while the children grow up half clothed and half fed.

When these things are known, it is scarcely to be wondered at that sometimes the poor peasant grows sullen and rebellious, and begrudges the great lord near by his splendid wealth and unstinted luxury.

But England has an empire large enough to give every one of her poor families an estate. Her homestead and emigration laws are most helpful and liberal. Under these circumstances we cannot wonder that so many of her subjects are turning their faces towards the lands of the setting sun.

Toronto, like St. John, is a city of American tendencies and sympathies. Loyal to the Crown, she is American in spirit. The boys hoped that American songs might be popular here, and that they might here give a concert that would be profitable.

"I like Toronto!" said Noble to Master Lewis. "Would it not be well to advertise our concert under the name of "The Old Songs of Canada and the States"?

"The songs of Mackay are not old," said Master Lewis. "Mackay himself is living. I think that 'The National Songs of the States and Canada' would be better. That name would properly include 'The Canadian Boat-Song,' 'The King's Son with his Silver Gun,' 'Dead Man's Isle,' and the English and French renderings of 'God Save the King.'"

"'Hail, Columbia!'" continued Master Lewis, "would be likely to awaken old memories and pictures of old associations here. Let me tell you its history more fully than Charlie has told it. It is associated with our nation's relations with France.

"'Hail, Columbia!' was written in the summer of 1798, at a moment when the United States seemed about to be drawn into a war with France, their old ally and friend. The American envoys sent out by President Adams with no other object than to restore a good understanding, were thought to have been grossly insulted by France. An army and a navy were in preparation. General Washington had accepted the chief command, with Alexander Hamilton as his second; and nothing was thought of but impending war.

"A vocalist by the name of Fox was about to have a benefit in Philadelphia, and, owing to the excitement that prevailed, the prospect of a good attendance was not encouraging. His benefit was announced for a Monday evening, and it was only on the Saturday previous that he had an idea for 'drawing a house.'

"One of his schoolfellows, Joseph Hopkinson, son of a distinguished father, had become himself a man of note in the intellectual circles of Philadelphia society. He was Vice-President of the American Philosophical Society, founded by Dr. Franklin and presided over by Thomas Jefferson. He was President of the Academy of Fine Arts, and somewhat noted for his poetical effusions.

"The vocalist, in his extremity, went to his old school-friend, and told him that he had little chance of a paying audience unless he could announce something new and striking in the way of a patriotic song, — a piece that could be sung by the whole company to an easy or familiar tune, like the 'President's March.' He added that the poets of the company had been trying to produce the required song, but had been unable to accomplish it.

"'I will try what I can do for you, said Hopkinson.

"The vocalist called the next afternoon, when the words were

ready for him; and he took them at once to a musician, who selected
and adapted to them an old and easy air. On Monday morning the
song was announced in the newspapers, and diligently rehearsed
upon the stage.

"A crowded house rewarded the efforts of the singer and the poet,
and the song was received with the greatest enthusiasm. The words
and music were at once published, and the piece was sung at every
patriotic gathering during that period of excitement.

"A particular circumstance added to its popularity, and was perhaps the true cause of its remaining for forty years not merely the
favorite national song, but the only composition that could be fairly
called by that name.

"During the first years of the revolutionary movement in France —
from 1789 to the execution of Louis XVI. and Marie Antoinette in
1793 — its progress was watched in America with an enthusiastic
approval of which we can now scarcely form an idea. But the execution of the king and queen checked the enthusiasm, and soon
divided the country into two parties on the subject, — one defending,
the other execrating, the conduct of the revolutionary leaders.

"At the height of the first excitement, while even the placid Washington was still in sympathy with the people of France, Addison's
famous old tragedy of 'Cato' was revived in Philadelphia. The curtain rose, and the whole company of actors, arranged in a semicircle
upon the stage, sang the national hymn of France, 'La Marseillaise,' —
a new composition then. The audience sprang to their feet and
joined in the chorus. The house presented a scene of excitement
without previous parallel in the staid city of Penn and Franklin.

"The audience called for a repetition of the inspiring song. It
was given as before, the people joining wildly in the chorus. It
seemed as if the people could not get enough of it. Even upon
us, who have been familiar with it from childhood, this wonderful
song has an effect unlike that of any other.

MARIE ANTOINETTE.

"The next evening, and every evening, as soon as the musicians came into the orchestra, the cry arose all over the house for 'La Marseillaise.' It was of no use to resist, for the people would listen to no other music. Generally the audience, or some part of it, would catch the spirit of the piece, and thunder out the chorus. It grew into a custom, and for three or four years the piece was sung every night. But as the guillotine in Paris quickened its activity, the enthusiasm of audiences abated.

"One night, during the patriotic fervor of 1798, soon after the arrival of ill-news from France, one man, upon hearing the usual faint demand for the 'Marseillaise,' ventured to dissent by hissing. At once the whole audience joined in one decisive and overwhelming hiss. The 'Marseillaise' was not played, and was never played again.

"It was at this time that the new song of 'Hail, Columbia!' made its great success. Never was a composition better timed. It immediately took the place of the banished 'Marseillaise,' and continued to be sung, as a rule, in all the places of amusement of the United States until about the year 1840.

"The introductory music was usually presented in the following order: an overture, followed by 'Hail, Columbia!' played several times, and then 'Yankee Doodle.'

"Joseph Hopkinson died at Philadelphia in 1842, aged seventy-two years. A few months before his death he placed on record the facts given above, and added:—

"'The object of the author was to get up an *American spirit*, which should be independent of, and above, the interest, passion, and policy of both belligerents, and look and feel exclusively for our honor and rights. No allusion is made to France or England, or the quarrel between them, or to the question which was most in fault in their treatment of us; of course, the song found favor with both parties, for both were American; at least, neither could disown the sentiments and feelings it indicated.'

" The following are the words of the song, as originally written at Philadelphia in 1798 : —

HAIL, COLUMBIA!

Hail, Columbia, happy land !
Hail, ye heroes ! Heaven-born band !
Who fought and bled in Freedom's cause,
Who fought and bled in Freedom's cause,
And when the storm of war was gone,
Enjoyed the peace your valor won.
Let independence be your boast,
Ever mindful what it cost :
Ever grateful for the prize,
Let its altar reach the skies.

  Firm, united, let us be,
  Rallying round our Liberty ;
  As a band of brothers joined,
  Peace and safety we shall find.

Immortal patriots ! rise once more,
Defend our rights, defend our shore ;
Let no rude foe with impious hand,
Let no rude foe with impious hand,
Invade the shrine where sacred lies
Of toil and blood the well-earned prize ;
While offering peace sincere and just,
In Heaven we place a manly trust
That truth and justice may prevail,
And every scheme of bondage fail.
  Firm, united, let us be, etc.

Sound, sound the trump of Fame !
Let Washington's great name
Ring through the world with loud applause,
Ring through the world with loud applause ;
Let every clime to Freedom dear
Listen with a joyful ear :
With equal skill and godlike power
He governs in the fearful hour
Of horrid war, or guides with ease
The happier times of honest peace.
  Firm, united, let us be, etc.

LOUIS XVI.

Behold the Chief who now commands,
Once more to serve his country stands, —
The rock on which the storm will beat,
The rock on which the storm will beat,
But armed in virtue firm and true ;
His hopes are fixed on Heaven and you.
When hope was sinking in dismay,
And gloom obscured Columbia's day,
His steady mind, from changes free,
Resolved on death or liberty.
Firm, united, let us be, etc.

"The song became the war-note of 1812, of the battle of Lake Erie, and the conflicts on the lakes and the British American border."

A lively interest in the concert was indicated as soon as the announcement of it was made in the papers. Master Lewis and the Class had personal interviews with several men of the press, and the boys were asked to sing at one of the Clubs, and did so; gaining thereby much free advertising by way of commendation in the local journals. Every seat in the hall was sold before the night of the concert.

"We shall not be taken by surprise by coming to an empty hall in Toronto," said Charlie Noble.

"No," said Master Lewis ; "but one cannot tell what surprises may happen to one at an exhibition. I once knew a soloist who was flattered by a large audience, but who was so overcome by the appreciation that his mind failed him, and he had to stop in the middle of his principal song."

"There is no danger of anything of that kind happening to us," said Charlie.

"But it might rain," said Robertson.

"Suppose it should ; we have sold the seats and got the money."

"Or there might be a fire "

"But we have got the money now."

The night was lovely, and the hall was crowded at an early hour.

The hall had not been used during the summer season. There was a curtain before the platform, and Charlie Noble thought it would be well to have it raised just as the Class began to sing the first song, which on this occasion was to be, " Cheer, boys, cheer."

The Class took their position on the platform. It was that of a crew of English sailors. Charlie gave the signal to the usher to raise the curtain, and the Class began the song lustily and heartily, —

> " Cheer, boys, cheer, the merry breeze is blowing,
> To wait us softly o'er the ocean breast ;
> The world shall follow in the path we 're going, —
> The star of empire glitters in the West."

At the end of the second line there was a most surprising and embarrassing *hitch* in the proceedings. The curtain went up about two feet, and would go no farther. The feet and legs of the boys were before the eyes of the audience, but their faces were in oblivion. A more ridiculous tableau could hardly be imagined.

The usher tugged away at the cords of the curtain. His efforts were too spasmodic under the excitement, and they broke. He sat down on the nearest seat, and wiped his face in despair.

The audience was too well bred for any coarse expression of ridicule, but there was a laugh in every one's face.

What would the singers do?

In the dilemma the chorus rang out behind the curtain, —

> " Cheer, boys, cheer, for country, mother country."

Not a voice faltered, and the boys' feet began to move in military precision to the rhythm of the chorus. The " boys" in the audience began to " cheer" indeed. The song went on without faltering ; the feet of the boys, which were almost the only objects in sight of the audience, joining in the ringing choruses.

At the end of the song the house rang with applause. The boys were recalled. They returned with firm step, behind the obstinate and mysterious curtain. They repeated the song, and were again as loudly applauded.

There was a broad space in front of the curtain, for the hall was not a theatre. In the anteroom were a drum and fife which the boys had used at a previous concert in " Yankee Doodle," and which they had brought for a like use now, should they have occasion to sing this song on a recall. .

The applause continued. The audience saw the ghostly feet disappear, but were presently surprised to hear the sound of drum and fife, and to see the boys marching into the room by a side door to the music of " Yankee Doodle."

The audience arose. Men waved their hats, and ladies their handkerchiefs, and the boys shouted. The Class marched coolly around the hall; then the boys mounted the platform in front of the curtain, and, facing the audience, made a very low bow.

The good-will and enthusiasm of the audience were completely won. The boys found themselves in an inspiring atmosphere, and were now doubly eager to sing their best.

"Cheer, boys, cheer," was followed by the original song of " Yankee Doodle," to the music of the drum and fife.

YANKEE DOODLE.

Dad and I went down to camp
  Along with Captain Goodwin,
Where we *see* the men and boys
  As thick as hasty *puddin'*

There was *Captain* Washington
  Upon *a strapping* stallion
A giving orders to his men ;
  I *guess* there was a million.

And then the feathers on his hat,
  They looked so tarnal *fine*,
I wanted peskily to get,
  To give to my Jemima.

And then they had a *swampin'* gun
  As big as log of maple,
On a *denced* little cart, —
  A load for father's cattle.

And every time they fired it off
  It took a horn of powder:
It made a noise like father's gun,
  Only a nation louder.

I went as near to it myself
  As Jacob's underpinnin',
And father went as near again, —
  I thought the deuce was in him.

Cousin Simon grew so bold,
  I thought he would have cocked it ;
It scared me so I shrinkèd off
  And hung by father's pocket.

And Captain Davis had a gun,
  He *kind a* clapped his hand on 't,
And stuck a crooked stabbing iron
  Upon the little end on 't.

And there I *see* a pumpkin shell
  As big as mother's basin ;
And every time they touched it off
  They scampered like the nation.

And there I *see* a little keg,
  Its head was made of leather;
They knocked upon 't with little sticks
  To call the folks together.

And then they'd *fife away like fun*,
  And play on *cornstalk* fiddles,
And some had *ribbons* red as blood
  All wound around their middles.

The troopers, too, would gallop up,
  And fire right in our faces ;
It scared me almost half to death
  To see them run such races.

Old Uncle Sam came there to change
  Some pancakes and some onions
For *'lasses cakes*, to carry home
  To give to his wife and young ones.

I *see* another *snarl* of men
  A diggin' graves, they told me. —
So *tarnal* long, so *tarnal* deep,
  They 'tended they should hold me.

They scared me so, I *hooked* it off,
  Nor slept, as I remember,
Nor turned about till I got home,
  Locked up in mother's chamber.

The old song was so heartily cheered that Charlie departed again from the programme, and the Class gave " The Battle of the Baltic " for English ears, and followed it with " The King's Son with the Silver Gun " for the French : —

    " Trois beaux canards
      S'en vont baignant !
  Fringue ! fringue sur l'aviron !
      Le fils du roi
      S'en va chassant.
  Fringue ! fringue sur la rivière !
  Fringue ! fringue sur l'aviron ! "

The concert was so popular and successful that it was repeated by request. The profits of the two concerts were large, and contributed almost enough to meet the amount needed to pay the expenses of the excursion of the five boys who needed such assistance.

" We have done well this time," said Charlie Noble, on leaving Toronto. " If we lack a few dollars, we will make up the amount when we return, by giving concerts of *Canadian* songs."

" Yes," said Master Lewis, " you have done *nobly*."

The boys collected many provincial French songs for use at home concerts, should they need them. Among these were " A la claire Fontaine," " Vive la Canadienne," " A Saint Malo," " Beau Port

de Mer," "Va, va, va," "P'tit Bonnet." But the song that they best
liked to sing together was the following, similar to the "King's Son,"
already mentioned. We give both words and music, but should explain that the narrative part is sustained by a single voice. It was
evidently written to be sung on a boat,—the refrain to the motion
of the oars.

EN ROULANT MA BOULE.

Derrièr' chez nous, y a-t-un étang,
En roulant ma boule.
Trois beaux canards s'en vont baignant,
Rouli, roulant, ma boule roulant.
En roulant ma boule roulant,
En roulant ma boule.

Trois beaux canards s'en vont baignant,
En roulant ma boule.
Le fils du roi s'en va chassant,
Rouli, roulant, ma boule roulant,
En roulant, etc.

Le fils du roi s'en va chassant,
En roulant ma boule,
Avec son grand fusil d'argent,
Rouli, roulant, ma boule roulant,
En roulant, etc.

TORONTO.

Avec son grand fusil d'argent,
      En roulant ma boule.
Visa le noir, tua le blanc,
Rouli, roulant, ma boule roulant,
        En roulant, etc.

Visa le noir, tua le blanc,
      En roulant ma boule.
O fils du roi, tu es méchant !
Rouli, roulant, ma boule roulant,
        En roulant, etc.

O fils du roi, tu es méchant !
      En roulant ma boule.
D'avoir tué mon canard blanc,
Rouli, roulant, ma boule roulant,
        En roulant, etc.

D'avoir tué mon canard blanc,
      En roulant ma boule.
Par dessous l'aile il perd son sang,
Rouli, roulant, ma boule roulant,
        En roulant, etc.

Par dessous l'aile il perd son sang,
      En roulant ma boule.
Par les yeux lui sort'nt des diamants,
Rouli, roulant, ma boule roulant,
        En roulant, etc.

Par les yeux lui sort'nt des diamants,
      En roulant ma boule.
Et par le bec l'or et l'argent,
Rouli, roulant, ma boule roulant,
        En roulant, etc.

Et par le bec l'or et l'argent,
      En roulant ma boule.
Toutes ses plum's s'en vont au vent,
Rouli, roulant, ma boule roulant,
        En roulant, etc.

Toutes ses plum's s'en vont au vent,
    En roulant ma boule.
Trois dam's s'en vont les ramassant,
Rouli, roulant, ma boule roulant,
        En roulant, etc.

Trois dam's s'en vont les ramassant,
    En roulant ma boule.
C'est pour en faire un lit de camp,
Rouli, roulant, ma boule roulant,
        En roulant, etc.

C'est pour en faire un lit de camp,
    En roulant ma boule.
Pour y coucher tous les passants,
Rouli, roulant, ma boule roulant,
En roulant ma boule roulant,
        En roulant ma boule.

The Class returned with a somewhat intelligent view of Canadian history, geography, and romance, with a real love for England's great province, and a purpose to make a more careful study of all that pertains to our hospitable neighbors beyond the boundaries of the St. Lawrence and the Lakes.

"Happy Canada!" there is a romance and a brightness about thee that the tourist can never forget; and, better than all, the scenery around Canadian homes is equalled by the greatness and the love of Canadian hearts.

The southern empire of France has gone, and a memory is all that remains of the splendid achievements of the French pioneers on the St. Lawrence and the Mississippi. The *Fleur-de-lis* is a ghost of the past. But the northern empire, under the Red Cross, remains as of old; and of no subjects of her crown may England be prouder, than of the hardy, honest, fruitful men of the North.

To visit the Canada of to-day is to gain moral help, courage, and strength.

The memory of a journey in summer through the grand water-ways of Canada can never be effaced. The mountain-walled rivers and lakes are as beautiful to-day as when they filled Champlain with wonder, and Allouez pursued the solitary trail by the blue inland seas, and Marquette first saw in the sand the footprints of the Illinois.

THE MEN OF THE NORTH.

I.

FIERCE as its sunlight, the East may be proud
Of its gay gaudy hues and its sky without cloud ;
Mild as its breezes, the beautiful West
May smile like the valleys that dimple its breast ;
The South may rejoice in the vine and the palm,
In its groves, where the midnight is sleepy with balm :
        Fair though they be,
        There 's an isle in the sea,
The home of the brave and the boast of the free !
Hear it, ye lands ! let the shout echo forth, —
The lords of the world are the Men of the North !

II.

Cold though our seasons, and dull though our skies,
There 's a might in our arms and a fire in our eyes :
Dauntless and patient, to dare and to do, —
Our watchword is " Duty," our maxim is " Through !"
Hardship and danger but nerve us the more
To rival the deeds of the true men of yore :
        Strong shall we be
        In our isle of the sea,
The home of the brave and the boast of the free !
Firm as the rock when the storm flashes forth,
We 'll stand in our courage — the Men of the North !

III.

Sunbeams that ripen the olive and vine,
In the face of the slave and the coward may shine ;
Roses may blossom where Freedom decays,
And crime be a growth of the sun's brightest rays.

Scant though the harvest we reap from the soil,
Yet Virtue and Health are the children of Toil;
      Proud let us be
      Of our isle of the sea,
The home of the brave and the boast of the free;
Men with true hearts, — let our fame echo forth, —
Oh, these are the fruit that we grow in the North!

MACKAY.

University Press: John Wilson & Son, Cambridge.

" Soon as the woods on shore look dim
We'll sing at Saint Anne's our parting hymn.
Row, brothers, row; the stream runs fast,
The rapids are near, and the daylight's past.

Canadian

Boat

Song

by

Thomas

Moore

The Old Church
of
St. Anne Canada

" Saint of this isle! hear our prayers!
Oy! grant cool heavens, and favouring airs.
Blow, breezes, blow; the stream runs fast,
The rapids are near, and the daylight's past. "

www.ingramcontent.com/pod-product-compliance
Lightning Source LLC
Chambersburg PA
CBHW060533030726
47498CB00004B/1184